Also by Janice Miller Potter

Meanwell

Psalms in Time

Thoreau's Umbrella

Janice Miller Potter

Fomite
Burlington, VT

Copyright © 2019 Janice Miller Potter
Cover image - Photo by Jan Fillem on Unsplash
Author Photo by Heather Potter

All rights reserved. No part of this book may be reproduced in any form or by any means without the prior written consent of the publisher, except in the case of brief quotations used in reviews and certain other noncommercial uses permitted by copyright law.

ISBN- 978-1-947917-27-9
Library of Congress Control Number: 2019945592

Fomite
58 Peru Street
Burlington, VT 05401
www.fomitepress.com

For Richard

*My life has been the poem I would have writ,
But I could not both live and utter it.*

–Henry David Thoreau

Contents

I.

Concord Born	3
A Little Book of Days	4
Chickens	6
The Red House on Lexington Road	7
Dame School	8
Cynthia	9
The Sabbath Hawk	10
Uncle Charles	11
John and Henry	13
Huckleberries	14
Aunt Hills and Bee Hives	15
The Rover	17
The Green Coat	19
Ways of Being Alone in College	21
The Privateer	22
Father	23
Shanty in the Irish Manner	24
The Sea Will Not Stagnate	25
Flogger Thoreau	27
The Knapsack	29

II.

Pencil Maker	33
At Cynthia Thoreau's Table	35
How Great Minds Quicken	37
This Double-Dealing Quacking World	39
Walking with Alcott	40
Margaret Fuller on Walden Pond	41
Tahatawan's Arrowhead	43
Schoolmaster in Search of a Schoolhouse	44
The Forerunner	46
Ellen Sewall	48
I Can Not Tell You Half I Have Enjoyed Here	49
John's Girl	51

Stoic	52
June and All	53
Scituate Beach	54
Star-Crossed Letters	56
The Husbandry Poet	57
Under the Cold Cold Moon	58
Bush	59
The Children	60
Lidian	61
The Budding Tree	63
Eleven Days to Eternity	64
Phantoms	65
An Eagle Wrestling the Wind	66

III.

A Wedding Garden	69
Beauty and the Beast	70
Winterfire 1842	72
A Leaf in Ice	73
Snuggery Blues	75
Thoreau in New York	76
Dear Lidian—	77
The Linen and Woolen Man	78
Among the Ruins	79
Making Pencils, Thoreau Discovers the Secret of Success	80
That Terrible Thoreau	81
Clapper and Bell	83
On Being Called a Sponge	85
The House on Texas Street	86
Concord Spring 1845	88
Directive	89
The Pines of Walden	90
To Those Who Are Not Ashamed of Economy	91
A Little Rumor like Salt	92
Thoreau's Umbrella	93

IV.

Starting for Conantum	97
Surveyor	98
Walking in Rainlight, Thoreau Considers His Eye	99
Birdland	100
An Arch over the Darker Gulf	101
From a Granite Ledge on Greylock, Thoreau Considers the Railroad	103
Loafing	104
Solitude	105
Therien/Thoreau	106
Sophia's Sleep	107
The Flute on the Pond	108
Who Will Pay the Ferryman?	109
Walden Sky Water	110
Confessions of a Nineteenth-Century Naturalist	111
The View from the Taffrail	112
A Funny Thing Happens on the Way to the Cobbler's Shop	113
The Picnic Grove	115
Ktaadn	116
Bee in a Jar	120
Man of the House	121
Morning Star	124
The Lovesong of Miss Sophia Foord	125
The Lecture Wars	129
On the Concord and the Merrimack	131
Thy Indelible Mild Eye Is My Sky	132
The Yellow House on Main Street	133

V.

Whitman's Room	137
The Irish Graveyard at Grampus Rock	140
Fire Island	142
Margaret's Ghost	146
On First Looking at Lake Champlain, Thoreau Sees Water	147
At the Cathedral of Notre Dame in Montreal	149
Wild Apples	150
Wild Man	151

In His Thirty-Fourth Year, Thoreau Hears the Music of Time	152
Snake Summer	154
Chess-Boxers	155
Thoreau Leaves the Party	156
The Quiet Man	157
The Moose Hunt	158
Fugitive Justice	159
The Brown Defense	162
Autumnal Tints	163
Cold	164
Minnesota	165
Wild Grapes	166
Up Country	167
Acknowledgments	169
About the Author	171

I.

I am like a feather floating in the atmosphere;
on every side is depth unfathomable.

–Henry David Thoreau

Concord Born

Independent of any neighbors
on the twelfth day of July in 1817,
the unpainted farmhouse on Virginia Road
blends with hayfields and hedgerows
on the fringe of Concord, Massachusetts.
Lately, at all hours of the day and night,
the windows of its upper rooms
have been flung wide open.
Expelling midsummer heat, they also
invite the least rustle of a cooling breeze,
the flittering sounds of high oak leaves,
the plaintive cries of phoebes in the eaves,
the cawing of crows over sun-scorched fields,
the moonlight reserve of a saw-whet owl.

Opened wide, his grandmother's windows
invite all nature in while he himself enters
the world expanding outward from Concord.
No one notices a sudden mistle of rain.
Above his own first cries, does he hear
the voice of a bobolink in the swaying hay?
Do his blue-gray eyes reflect weathers
painted on moving skies beyond the sash?
Does the giant American elm,
planted a generation ago, cast its vague
shadow of depression, fleetingly,
across his sensitive infant eyes?
His grandmother cleanses his pink limbs
of placental blood and blossomy snow,
then places him in his mother's arms.
Her dictatorial fingers direct his tiny
toothless mouth to her ample breast,
where he learns his first lesson as her son.

A Little Book of Days

One day a mad hen knocks him down.
Staring up into her orange feathers
and scaly yellow claws, he wonders
if her squawk is the wrath of God
his aunts caution him about.
Thrashing him—but whatever for?
One day his big brother John smashes
a bladder of water onto the hearth.
At the burst, his whole body hiccups.
One day he falls down the stairs and faints.
He holds his breath for so long that
it takes two pails of water to wake him.
One day he finds a cow inside the house,
helping herself to a pumpkin.
He likes how her dripping mouth
gouges and chews the orange flesh,
then litters moon-shapes on the floor.

One day when no one is around
he hoists up a heavy axe,
and tries to swing it as Father does.
He chops off a toe.
At first it seems a thing he's done
to some other creature.
He flushes in amazement.

Will he later recall his mother's scream
or his father's curse?
Will he recall, too, the combustion
of aunts exploding around him?
What happened to the severed toe
of two-year old Henry Thoreau?
Can his mother have tossed it to compost,
like a maggotty turnip?
Did she bury it like a dead cat?

With a suitable shudder of ceremony?
Perhaps Father hurled the bloody thing
far across some hayfield
to let nature claim her ounce.
The final resting place of the toe
remains cloaked in mystery.
It disappeared, but he knows
it went somewhere.

Not knowing everything is
knowing something,
in the book of this inquisitive child
whom nature, like a snake,
both horrifies and fascinates.
Thunderstorms frighten him so
that he cowers in a darkened room,
pretending to be sick,
until safe in Father's arms.
Night after night he lies awake
in the trundlebed beside his brother.
"Why, Henry dear, don't you go to sleep?"
whispers Mother, peering into his eyes,
now blue-silver pools in the moonlight.
"Mother, I have been looking through the stars
to see if I could see God behind them."

Such thoughts this child unearths,
as rare and hard as flinten arrowheads.
Still, he puzzles at the unseen power
that makes things be things.
On June 24, 1819, Mother calls him
to her bedside to touch a mop of hair
who will be christened Sophia.
His huge eyes glisten
at this new phenomenon,
and he is glad without knowing why or how.

Chickens

One yellow, the other black.
Henry has watched their warm eggs wobble
and soon crack,
        as he imagines
                broken hearts do

when Mother gossips about
Daniel Webster's unrequited love for
her maiden sister Louisa.
        But he's not sorry,
                for chicks flopped out.

When no one's looking, he
holds them to his breast
and pets their pin-feathery heads,
        and invents silly names
                like Heeby and Jeeby.

As fat hens, they're his followers,
as he sings quietly to them, sowing grain
and seeds of wisdom in his way.
        Not too obvious, but still
                not ashamed.

Father says you should show those fat birds
to the innkeeper and see what
he'll give you for them. So, proud
        of his hen-husbandry, Henry
                packs them up.

While he waits to see, the innkeeper whisks
a commotion of wings from the crate.
Wrings yellow. Wrings black.
        Henry doesn't budge.
                Utters not a sound.

The Red House on Lexington Road

John builds a log raft from kindling beside the stove
and gets warned to move that mess off the rug.
But Henry rides on Mother's hip.

Helen sets her flowery china cups on a little green table
and softly reads her dolls a picture book.
But Henry waves from Mother's hip.

Tending Father's store, Mother darts here and there,
talking nonstop, while gentry ladies wait like cold porridge.
Henry smiles from Mother's hip.

Living in Grandmother's red house on Lexington Road,
Father does not talk much, but Mother's loud talk
makes a rivery stream in her neck.

Henry buries his nose in the milky smell of her breast
when Aunt Sarah Thoreau comes and talks on and on about
fourteen months and high time. Glaring at him.

Finally Aunt Sarah herself takes the bull by the horns.
Hauling him off, she stands the child in the center of the rug.
She commands him. Giddily, Henry walks for the first time.

Walking means standing on round feet with toes turned up,
not down. On bare feet, the rug feels like a woolly-worm.
Henry sits down often, then stubbornly rolls up again.

One day Mother puts a bright red flannel dress on him
and plants him outside. Toddling fast through the ragged grass,
he hears a skeptical snort just before a cow tosses him high.

Dame School

His apron strings tied to Miss Wheeler's knee,
little Henry patiently tells her his A B C's.
In spite of having learned them quicker than
a spit in his old left-behind Boston nursery.
But at Phoebe Wheeler's on Walden Street,
shaded by great buttonwood trees, is where
Concord's nicest infant school is kept. Proud
Cynthia Thoreau *must* put her children there.
Obliging, Henry often tires and veers to sleep.
His soft lashes flutter over his pond-blue eyes.
Then Miss Phoebe carries him to a corner bed
where he naps in public, like his Uncle Charles.

Some days, he grows churlish and disobedient.
He upsets Miss Phoebe, who has nothing more
in her bag of tricks than sternly shutting him
inside her stairway closet for his punishment.
Alone in the dark, Henry listens to the rhythm
of his breath. Ah huff ah huff. A tingly rasp
saws inside his chest. He is not frightened.
Trees and rocks, fishes and deer come to him.
But Miss Phoebe suffers awful pangs of guilt.
One day, while she uncramps his stubby legs
and brushes spiders from his hair, he asks
a serious question: "Who owns all the land?"

Cynthia

Lady of wild things,
lover of the woods and the chase over mountains,
huntswoman of the gods
and twin sister of Phoebus, that brilliant singer with his golden lyre,
that laureled boy who gentles even the field-mouse,
and loves the crow as well as the dolphin—
what dominion has Cynthia.

Fierce and revengeful
as her birthplace on Mount Cynthus on Delos, she slays
with silver arrows, as sharp as icy hail piercing a maiden spring.
Against consolation, or for it,
the passionate adore her in all phases of blue and gold.
Mood-shifts, from cow's horn to milky orb.
For unlike any other power in heaven and earth,
she is the protectress of dewy youth,
of the dark cypress and the leaping deer
of unspeakable night-thoughts and illuminations.
Flashing through the blackened forest,
making all beautiful with her light,
at the end of the day
she nurtures the wilder urge in a sunless world
that, yet, is fair and green.

Little Buddha, Henry meditates on
his mother as she sails about house and store.
As she walks her children through fields and woods,
along streams loud with hyla in spring,
loud with water gurgling under ice in winter.
All the while, her running commentary
blends with his quiet absorption in her presence.
Her voice, the clear river running.
Himself, the wild iris nodding cordially beside her.
With hot childish passion, he loves nature
because he loves Cynthia.

The Sabbath Hawk

The dreadful day scourges his mind
weekly, making it see
the red-marbled ochre under a tomahawk
he'd pried from the earth.

His slender fingers were as eager
as the whitish-pink worms
that had squirmed from their chilled stupor
to stretch and pour down hatches

tunneled by themselves
for just such occasions of escape.
He, too, would escape this churchy day of dread,
a day carved out of clouds and fire.

No glib music or book on this day,
no gleeful romp through the garden to the woods.
No worm, no stone, no soil,
no wild rustle of young green leaves

may burst out for sheer combustible livingness
on this corseted day. Worm that he is,
he glides up to the attic to revel in solitude.
Through a high open window, he leans and observes

a mass of purple martins sling across the sky,
then whip into one household.
The pursuing shadow of a marsh hawk lights on
his heart with dreadful joy.

Uncle Charles

Uncle Charles was born with wandering feet,
say his kindlier critics.
Uncle Charles lives everywhere and nowhere,
mostly tossing his knapsack under his mother's spare bed
until Mary Jones Dunbar is dead,
possibly of filial adhesion.
Then Uncle Charles moves into his sister Cynthia's home
until the itch gets to his feet some night;
and before morning the shabby knapsack is gone.
Someone may report a sighting of Uncle Charles
shambling along the coast of Maine.
Someone may catch a glimpse of a Charles-like figure
cutting hay up in northern Vermont.
Someone will swear they saw Uncle Charles ensconced
in a canoe, shooting the rapids on the Merrimack.
Sightings of Uncle Charles provide fodder for his myth,
devoured like Classical Greek literature
by his hero-hungry nephews.
But just when John Thoreau rubs his hands and grins,
he finds the Concord Odysseus
asleep by the stove in the morning!

Eating his hot bread, Henry stares at
the side-turned soles, puddled with holes,
as if all conventions have drained away through them.
Unperturbed by an audience, Uncle Charles snores on.
The sight of a man asleep, snoring, seems to Henry
a spectacle of the commonest sense.
Far from the dullest thing he can imagine,
it sparks his wonderment at dreams.
Henry knows that an iron skillet dropped near his thrown-back head
will not wake Uncle Charles while such dreams
are galloping through the gates of horn or ivory.
Henry has seen Uncle Charles asleep on his feet.
Transfixed, he has stood beside the bedroom mirror

while the sleeping Uncle Charles drew a straight-razor down his lathered jaw.
On Sundays, trotted out to hear the Reverend Ezra Ripley,
Henry is deliciously aware that
Uncle Charles has been made to sprout potatoes in the cellar
to keep awake and, somehow, keep the Sabbath.
Henry would like to sprout potatoes, too.
To sit on a stool in Hades, feeling with forefinger and thumb
for the starry, white sprouts on earthy flesh
and finding sprouted stars with comet-tails
trailing over baskets full of potato-y earthen orbs.
Sitting in church, he dreams
of scattering troves of those stars to nearsighted chickens,
who never look skyward.
But in his mother's house, so far, he is not allowed
to act like pagan Uncle Charles.

Then—by fate or predestination—Uncle Charles
turns out to be none other than
the Redeemer of the impecunious Thoreaus!
No one can say exactly how it happens, for
that is the mystery.
Only those thin soles may hold a clue.
Wandering through Bristol, New Hampshire, his sore feet stumble on
a terrific mine of plumbago—
graphite, so pure and ripe for speculation that
Uncle Charles pulls off the one practical act of his life:
he stakes a claim.
And with high, sweet talk,
he lures John Thoreau into Concord for good
to become a silent partner in the firm of Dunbar & Stow.
Soon it will be simply John Thoreau & Co.,
pencil-makers.

John and Henry

While John perches on the schoolhouse fence
telling wild stories and jokes,
other boys roll in the grass, exaggerating split sides.
At recess they all follow John
and do whatever thing John decides to do.
Why? Because John horse-laughs bawdily and loves
to tease and play the clown.
And John plays every game the best.
He can crack-the-whip or chase-the-hoop better
than any boy around. And even when
he falls, he roars with laughter.
As if the world's a Concord plum,
and all his own.

Stupid.
The Judge.
The fine scholar with the big nose.
Whatever they call Henry will not make him cry,
or fight, or play their game.
Accused, once, of stealing a knife, he coolly replies,
"I did not take it."
Specially asked to play with Mrs. Hoar's children, he disappears
simply because "I did not want to."
Waiting on the sidelines, he quietly watches other boys
until in his own good time, John calls it quits.
When the two of them can go home
and be brothers again.

Huckleberries

On Nashawtuc Hill wild huckleberries
ripen on an arc of summer heat,
continuing to laze through September.
Their leaves collect the sun.
Their roots drink deeply of the rain
before it can vanish.

Tied against his side, the hand-ring
of the milk pail rasps a confidence
as he drops berries into the drum.
At first they utter metallic
declarations. Then, contented sighs
like the rhythm of his breath.

Nashawtuc Hill bleeds violet
into his hands and lips, washes away
martinet time. Though his deftness translates
to pudding at noon. In truth, countless
huckleberry hours amass the spirit
of his lives to come, one world at a time.

Aunt Hills and Bee Hives

At their genteel boardinghouse on Concord Square,
Henry's Thoreau aunts, Elizabeth and Sarah, bluntly state:
No ruffians allowed.
In the kitchen, Aunt Betsey wets the sugar spoon
before scrunching it into the sugar bowl for her guests.
When Henry asks why, she takes a lofty tone and cites
the universal need for economy.
But everyone in Concord knows that
sugar stuck to a spoon won't fall into the cups.

Other Thoreau aunts, Maria and Jane, keep addresses
in Boston and Cambridgeport.
But, really, they are moving by inches into Henry's house.
Aunt Jane, a pudgy old child, plays Jacob's Ladder with the boys
while angular Aunt Maria snaps "causes" from her traveling bag.
She rails on Abolition and the Rights of Man.
At her sharp voice, his ears ring. She sounds like a Citizen of the Revolution
with her fervid denunciations. Perhaps she will call for the Widow.
He listens closely.

After his doughty aunts Maria, Elizabeth, and Jane
march away from gentle Reverend Ripley's peaceful Congregation
to join the Trinitarian fire-and-brimstoners,
his mother Cynthia hesitates. A doctrinal schism has split
the town of Concord. Should she go, or stay? Uncertainly, she goes.
Only to be black-balled by the preacher.
Loitering nearby, Henry observes the queer contortion of her face
as she stands before a rain-struck parlor window.
Wordless, he shares her wounded silence.

Overnight, then, his mother's house turns into a beehive.
If her sisters-in-law can rake in cash from boarders,
she can do them one better. Of course her own sister,
Louisa Dunbar, stays free. And that is right and just; for
prim Aunt Louisa is the unrequited love of Daniel Webster!

But plenty of paying transients file through.
Mrs. Joseph Ward and daughter Prudence roost for life,
gabbling all over the house with Cynthia. Henry's sister Sophia says
it's "enough to drive a man to Nova Zembla for quiet."

The Rover

If success in life for the boys of Concord Academy
can be dreamt of—and that is a big if—
they will include an Attorney General in Grant's Cabinet;
a founder of the Republican Party and U. S. Marshall
who will protect Lincoln at Gettysburg;
a Solicitor General for the War Department during the Civil War;
and sundry judges, lawyers, senators, and congressmen.
Who are these would-be agents of government?
Who is Lincoln? Who is Grant?
What constitutes a Republican?
What awful knell sounds in the words "Civil War"?
Can a future be predicted like a bank of storms beyond distant mountains?

At eleven, Henry feels only the tangible moment.
A wooden plank near a gritty hearth warms his cheek
as he lies, conjuring something to write for Phineas Allen, Preceptor.
He rolls over and carefully forms a large, rounded script
with a pencil from his father's shop:
"There are four seasons in a year, Spring, Summer, Autumn, and Winter.
I will begin with Spring."
Ice thaws, fruit swells, brooks freeze.
Slowly, the seasons wheel.
"The birds whith visited us in Spring are now retireing to warmer countries. . . ."
The present moment is real,
dancing on a pin.

Henry leaves little impression on his schoolmates.
But after his last quarter at Concord Academy,
surely Preceptor Allen agrees with the universal truth of his words,
"Next comes Summer."
Lying in his rowboat, Henry lets the *Rover* float
across Walden Pond at the will of any wind that skims its surface.
Through half-closed eyes, he senses dapplings of sun and cloud
over his slim body as he enters the realm of true dream.
Into the womb of Walden, he sails inwardly, and more inwardly.

He is carried through a dark vortex
to a place where the boat touches sand, and he is aroused.
He watches himself rise from the boat like another being.

The Green Coat

Nothing changes. Clockwork days pass,
bracketed by prayers at dawn and twilight
in the mind-numbing, nut-freezing chapel.
Rolls and coffee, rolls and tea.
Dinner with meat at noon. Nothing
varies. Lectures read. Regurgitations spat out.
A cackle or a hoot before the study-bell.
Dead quiet.

Fledgling Harvard men flit about
in their prescribed soft-woolen black coats,
looking as smart as their wealthy fathers
can make them. Garnering points
for required attendance of chapel and class,
and for recitations and essays turned in
(no matter how vacant),
Harvard men are used to success.

If a neophyte dares to question,
the professor drily frowns, then continues
to read his lecture before a silent class.
"Discussion" is simply talking out of turn.
It is the Harvard way. A wonder, then,
a petition circulates against the marking rules
of President Quincy. But when it does,
one signature reads: *Henry D. Thoreau.*

Signed while wearing his infamous green coat,
quickly a running entertainment
among bored and boorish Harvard men.
Why does it not amaze that home sweetens
in his mind? His first October, as hills blaze,
he walks the twenty-some miles to Concord.
Both feet blister so badly,
he limps the last slow miles in his stockings.

You wonder about that chopped-off toe.
Is its phantom in his "grave Indian stride,"
goofily imitated by classmate Weiss?
Limping home, a reverie hangs on him,
like his homemade clothes. Green as grass,
his mother's cut-down coat must survive Harvard.
Will it stake him to shame forever? He disagrees.
Whatever its color, a coat is a coat.

Ways of Being Alone in College

Fall in love with fifty-thousand volumes within four walls.
Or at least as goodly a number of them as
you can devour, holed up in a dusty corner, alone
in the brilliance of Chaucer, Shakespeare, Milton. Indeed all
the poets, from Homer to the Romantics.
Milk their essence clean, draw out fine strands of genius,
fill page after page, to keep them close forever,
inside your commonplace book.

When not curiously dismembered, mind from body,
during a saturnalia in the library, slip quietly away, alone,
to wander through the fields of Cambridge
and along the banks of the Charles. There, despite the presence
of others like yourself, discover the moistly-penned, flourishing book
of Nature. The animate nest of a weasel in a hollow apple tree
will part you from yourself daily, for a whole winter.
A flicker's nest will thrive in a grove of the college yard
until your roommate destroys it.
        For all the world, the more you observe,
the more you are diminished. You pass for nothing.
Nature has swallowed what was you.

The Privateer

In 1773 the sea swallows and expels Jean Thoreau,
born in St. Helier on the sea-swept Isle of Jersey,
son of a Huguenot wine merchant from Tours.

From the surrounding sea, thunder resonates, claiming
Jean's birthright. What island boy can ever resist
the coil of persistent waves, the sand's yielding to naked feet?

The urnlike sea holds the ash of many such lovers, lured
by lust into privateering, then buckled under the sea's rage.
Had the boy drowned, what then? *Mais non.*

Shipwrecked, starved bag of bones, he is rescued by
a miracle ship. A sea-change that brings him to Boston
without any intention on his part of going there.

Good with his hands, he works in a sail loft and as a cooper.
When war breaks out, he serves under Paul Revere, privateers
again, and shares booty from the *Minerva Cartet*.

He starts a shop on Boston's Long Wharf, his entire stock
being a hogshead of sugar. The enterprise prospers.
Proudly, he moves up to King Street, with partners.

He marries Jennie Burns, a Scottish Quaker, and fathers ten
(one of whom is John Thoreau) before his wife is spent.
Remarried, he buys the Colonial Inn on the Concord square.

But he's forty-seven and tubercular. He catches a cold
while patrolling the riotous streets of Boston in a storm.
Sixteen years before Henry's birth, his grandfather dies of rain.

Father

Sentiment Father tenderly loves
flows from his plangent flute, from breath
as invisible as himself. Such beauty,
to him, he would weep if he dared.
Instead he lays his flute away.
In a dim corner, he opens some book
and slowly turns page over page,
rowing through a listless Eden.

Obliquely, Henry watches him
sit by the stove in his little shop,
glancing up to gossip amiably
with some loiterer. Peaceful,
ordinary music fills his greeting.
Henry would cry at him,
in anguish, if only he could look
his father in the eye.

Mother flies in, twittering
like a nightingale to her hidden mate.
Henry wills her treble notes
to his private music, cosseted
within the breath of his own flute.
When Father pushes up from his chair
to be caught in her arms,
he stands a head lower than his wife.

Shanty in the Irish Manner

Shanties with straw beds and a few tin pots
smoldering in rings of stone
litter the woods between Concord and Boston.
Any respectable passerby will at first startle at this gone-to-earth sign
of the utter shabbiness of humanity.
A bedraggled woman with a ratty child dragging on her teat.
A man in corduroy hauling poached tinder on his back.
Under his breath, a buck like Ellery Channing will mutter, "Patrick."
On the Cliffs of Moher or in the woods of Massachusetts,
this is hard cheese.
Though boys have patched together such huts in the woods
for as long as boys have played survival games.

When Harvard classes end in the spring of 1837,
Charles Stearns Wheeler throws up a shanty in the Irish manner,
with bunks of straw, on the shores of Flint's Pond,
near his family's home in Lincoln.
For six humid weeks, he and his friend Henry Thoreau
camp at the hut and pass the time as they will,
given any choice at all—
reading, sleeping, loafing—relaxing the wooden limbs
they had acquired at Harvard.
Undomestic, Charles and Henry boil no stew and scatter no pots;
they eat their meals at the Wheeler table.

Nevertheless, a decent passerby might scoff,
"Damned Irish."

The Sea Will Not Stagnate

Oyster pies, mock turtle soup, turkey, pig, and squabs
are gobbled by rowdy graduates on the July 18 Class Day,
while Thoreau sleeps peacefully on his bed of straw

in Wheeler's shanty by Flint's Pond. Dreaming,
perhaps, a "true" dream: Braiding the hushed flow
of the river with pickerel and regal water-snakes.

At the 1837 Harvard Commencement on August 30,
he shows up to be awarded "the old joke of a diploma."
Later he quips: "Let every sheep keep but his own skin."

But the day is climactic for his mother and his aunts,
especially as he's been assigned to give a speech
touting "The Commercial Spirit of Modern Times."

Instead, he excoriates American businessmen
for "a blind and unmanly love of wealth" and gross
selfishness in patriotism, religion, and home-lives.

Scanning a stormy sea of wealthy potential donors,
President Quincy fidgets at his shiny black robe.
The young rascal's voice continues to rise:

"The sea will not stagnate, the earth will be as green
as ever, and the air as pure" without the greedy rich.
(Bursar Farwell resolves to check Thoreau's bill.)

A decent life, "more wonderful than convenient,"
should be enjoyed by *all* persons. Here, the wags grin
at his infamous green coat. Others solemnly nod.

The thatch under the mortarboard flaps on, correcting
God, no less—calling for one day of labor and six of rest,
in which to imbibe the "sublime revelations of nature"!

Skipping Mr. Quincy's levee with sparkling punch,
Henry lights out of Harvard. The next day, R. W. E.
declares the intellectual independence of America.

Flogger Thoreau

The new master of Concord's Central School
savors the coolness of the room before pupils arrive.
His gray-blue eyes travel to the windows
where the schoolyard maples celebrate in a perpetual recess,
their hues of yellow and red glowing bolder each day
against a deep blue sky.
Of the four roads open to a college man—
the ministry, the law, medicine, and teaching—
teaching is his choice by default.
Two weeks in, he's a full-blown revolutionary.
> He wants children to question and compare original ideas,
> He wants them to conjecture and experiment before drawing conclusions.
> He does not want them to memorize or recite like puppets.
> He does not want to beat them into compliance.

He stands exactly opposed to normal school practice.

When Deacon Ball of the school committee drops in,
the tiny schoolroom is boiling over with noise.
Fifty-two pupils in all shapes and sizes are supposedly engaged
in the exciting discovery of what a gerund does,
or how less can be more. But a rude, loud racket is surging up
from a gang of hulking farm-boys, present by force.
Guffawing, burping, and sniggering at the slender young master,
they swagger for a clique of responsive girls.
Aghast, Deacon Ball calls the rookie outside and demands
that he either flog the students, or "the school would spoil."

Mortified, Thoreau bursts in, randomly calls out names,
both innocent and guilty, and ferules every one.
Blotched with red, his mother's own housemaid's face is
covered with tears of shock and hurt.
Lumpy Daniel Potter is so mad that he vows to whip Thoreau,
when he grows up.
By dusk of that very evening,
rather than compromise his principles,

Thoreau resigns his first job.
The victims learn the cruelest lesson—about injustice.
But what does the trauma teach Deacon Ball?
> *This young man is very odd.*

Reaching man's estate, Daniel shakes his lumpy head and says,
"Why, Henry Thoreau was the kindest hearted of men."
And shakes his head again.

The Knapsack

Handing off his letter of resignation to Nehemiah Ball,
who opens the door with a half-cracked look in his eye—

the eye snaps like a boiled egg when he sees it's Thoreau—
at first feels like a rush of freedom to a manacled slave.

Then he learns the hard way how scarce teaching jobs are.
What sort of letter would old Ball have given him anyhow?

Sheepish, he angles for his mother's comfort under the guise
of asking advice. Cynthia never fails a lavish fuss over him.

But now she lashes out: He can just buckle on his knapsack
and hit the road. Bonnet-ribbons quaking, she flounces off.

Tears spring to his large eyes. He feels whipped like a child
caught stealing a forbidden sweet. In humiliation he weeps

until Helen puts her arm around him and says, "No, Henry,
you shall not go: you shall stay at home and live with us."

II.

There is no remedy for love but to love more.

–Henry David Thoreau

Pencil Maker

Working with his father conjures
pleasant musks of sweat, as calming to him
as the scent of a companion nag
in the nostrils of an Arabian racehorse.
In comforting silence,
they mix graphite with bayberry wax,
glue, and spermaceti.
He presses the grit into greasy paste,
then warms it over a fire.
With care, he pours it into a narrow
groove prepared by his father.
A pencil good enough to write with if
you don't mind brittle grease.

In the Harvard Library, a Scottish encyclopedia
explains how the incomparable Fabers of Germany
bake lead with fine Bavarian clay—
the same clay imported to Taunton, Massachusetts
by the Phoenix Crucible Company.
With shadows dancing around a yellow lamp,
Henry's heart leaps at the thought of
unwrapping a body of Teutonic clay.
Then the Thoreaus learn that this foreign stuff
requires a finer and harder lead-dust
than any they possess to integrate.
Gray hair askew, Father tries to think.
Finally it comes to him.
Let Henry *invent* a way to capture the dust.

A churn-like chamber rises seven feet
to a closed box with an inner shelf.
Wound up to run like clockwork,
internal millstones grind down the gritty lead
the way a clock grinds time.
As in a fairy-tale, only the finest dust

is carried on a draft to the towering height.
There, it lodges on the shelf to await the hands—
and lungs—of the pencil maker.
Too close to purchase a patent,
the Thoreaus padlock windowless sheds,
where pure lead-dust rises
in so fine a splendor that it outdoes
Munroe, Dixon, all rivals, to produce
the best pencil in America—the Thoreau.

At Cynthia Thoreau's Table

Feathery green decades on, the walnut tree
endures an untimely death
in a dining table with two broad, dark leaves that can,
but will not, drop. He hopes.

Since childhood, he has counted his family
seated around the walnut table.
Making lists has always comforted him, keeping things—
and people—where they belong.

Mother shreds Lidian Emerson's white linen cap
with ridicule. Nunnish. Pseudo-Puritanical.
At the same time she heaps Father's blue plate
with dollops of creamed potatoes and succotash.

Silent and subdued, Father passes each dish
to John, who spoons the steaming medley of beans and corn
onto his own plate without losing the balance
of a very tall tale he is building.

Laughter all around. Beginning to ask
if John has written down his far-fetched stories,
Henry is drowned in a flood of babble
from his mother's lips. He stops and waits.

Patiently, he attends her loved lips,
observing a foolish spittle dancing before them.
Helen quietly smiles at her plate.
In a complicity with the damask tablecloth,

her checkered skirt falls across his knee.
Their peculiar weightlessness comforts him.
If words could tell, Sophia would.
If he could ask, she would expatiate on love.

Forcefully, like their mother, but with wisdom.
Even so, he is filled.
Laying aside his spoon, he imagines
the walnut leaves span and float as on summer air.

How Great Minds Quicken

Dark and plain at seventeen,
Sophia delights in her brother's silvery thoughts
as trumpeted by handsome Mr. Emerson.
At a Concord lyceum, she brushes aside a puff of jet hair,
the better to catch the lilt of the orator's voice.
Like a French-lace doily pinned with a cameo,
her white collar stands askew, matching her roiled emotions.
Almost prettily, her black eyes flash
when she fancies the speaker is pelting the crowd
with Henry's ideas:

What is the meaning of existence?
Where shall we go to seek an answer to this question?
Impotent minds probe the carrion of the past.
But the independent mind cultivates its own secret garden,
turning its rich, dark soil to reveal the deep source
of all human understanding.
Here, buried within, lies the meaning of all life,
continually quickening—and mirrored in small and vast Nature.
On and on, Henry's thoughts. . . .

Tickled, Sophia tells her boarder Lucy Jackson Brown,
who tells her sister Lydia—Lidian—
who tells her own Mr. E.
what Sophia's mother, Mrs. Thoreau,
has rattled along with the china cups and saucers
to anyone who will listen:
    How much Mr. Emerson does talk like my Henry!
Sapient Sophia digs up one of his old college papers
and sees that it passes from Lidian's slender hand
to her husband's writing table.

Brushing past the throbbing lilacs
near the big white house on Lexington Road
on Sunday, April 9, 1837, Henry absorbs

a momentum from their vigorous scent that pervades
his unpretentious words with Emerson.
That night, the great man wonders again and again
how this phenomenon whom he's invited into his life
has evolved out of the meanness
of cedar-pencil shavings and winnowings of gossip.

This Double-Dealing Quacking World

> *How comic is simplicity*
> *in this double-dealing quacking world.*
>   *–Ralph Waldo Emerson*

Walking out with Mr. Emerson
to the Cliffs on dew-heavy mornings,
to Walden Pond on leaf-canopied afternoons,
he bathes in a glow of approval.

Unconsciously he lengthens his stride
to accommodate the taller man's gait;
and he is amazed to hear his own voice
silver slightly in imitation of his friend.

Watchful Concord takes note and enjoys
many a sly snicker and heartier snort:
That worthless Da-a-vid Henry Thoreau,
he's even getting up a nose like Emerson's.

His old Harvard classmate, James Lowell,
sent down for misconduct, takes it out:
Why, the fellow so apes Emerson's talk that,
with eyes shut, one couldn't tell them apart.

Quips and quacks fly, bitter, high and low.
Disgusted, Thoreau rails at a careless Creation
for making the nature of the earth beholden
to a world of society that is worth so little.

Walking with Alcott

Even the rats and mice make their nests in him.
—Henry David Thoreau

Every fence rail, every stump
invites those buttocks to rest,
assisting his nibs to speechify.
Impossible to walk and to talk
at once when so full of straw
theories that the rats and mice
build their frowzy nests in him.
Thoreau fights a mean impulse
to cushion him in poison oak.
He likes Alcott. But never again
will he expect to walk with him.
Of an evening, he'll call, when
those buttocks are safely stowed
on the shabby horsehair sofa.
Where, unhindered by exertion,
talk may sprint down any path.

Margaret Fuller on Walden Pond

With rhythm akin to classical poetry,
he plies his long, self-made oars.
She braces her spine against the gunwale
in the pose of a ready woman
with convenient moonlight coming on.
Once, when his oars delve the air
just before their silent thrust,
she spies a pelt of hair on his arm.

As her gaze fastens on the animal
protruding from rolled sleeves,
his arm withdraws from her.
She sighs. It is all in the rhythm
of rowing, all an obvious metaphor
for sex. Carefully, she adjusts
a forebraid along her round ear
and goes on talking of Goethe.

Later she writes her brother about
that moonlit night on Walden Pond.
The song of the whippoorwill,
taught to her by Thoreau. A man
who filled her senses, like the heady
scent of mock orange solemnly
brushing their faces as they floated by.
As ephemeral as herself and Thoreau.

Later still she demands revisions or
rejects every poem he sends to *The Dial*.
Behind her back, he will scoff at her
romantic tome, *Summer on the Lake*.
But once, during a visit to Staten Island,
he will loosen his tight purse-strings
and gallantly pay for the carriage
she has ordered but does not ride.

If they play at being oil and water
to one another, so much the more
titillating to the old ladies of Concord.
Then the rogue ruins the fun when
one confronts him with the tale:
*"No, in the first place, Margaret Fuller is
not fool enough to marry me. And second,
I am not fool enough to marry her."*

Tahatawan's Arrowhead

After his twentieth birthday,
during the humid Massachusetts high summer,
Thoreau strolls out to the mouth of Swamp Bridge Brook
with his brother. Now that John and he are home again,
they become as inseparable as boys.

Spilling over the path, rich jewelweed
masses around them like a school of goldfish.
Joe-pye weed sprays dusty pink florets at their faces,
while milkweed stiffens with pale leaves to shield
the pods that will explode in autumn.

Thoreau stops short near the brow of a hill
that serves as a high bank on the Concord River.
Waving his long arms, he regresses into boyish drama:
*"There on Nawshawtuct was their lodge, the rendezvous of the tribe,
and yonder, on Clamshell Hill, their feasting ground. . . .*

Here stood Tahatawan; and there is Tahatawan's arrowhead."
They drop to a spot of ground and sit,
cross-legged, in imitation of Indian tales they've heard.
Reaching for a random stone, Thoreau
picks up the most perfect arrowhead he's ever seen.

Schoolmaster in Search of a Schoolhouse

We are all schoolmasters and our schoolhouse is the universe.
—Henry David Thoreau

He refuses to whip rowdy children.
Instead he calls himself their learning-partner,
no doubt to excuse loafing with them around the woods and streams.
In Concord he gets away with two weeks
before the schoolboard chairman gets after him.
Like a madman, he flogs lambs and goats alike
then hurls his resignation into the pie-eyed face of the chairman,
who is rousted from sleep in his worsted nightshirt.
No schoolboard will touch him now.

Finally, in June 1838, his mother takes pity on him
and lets him open a school in her parlor.
After all, what with her female-abolitionist boarders, the Wards,
a bevy of spinster-aunts from both sides
including Aunt Louisa Dunbar, beloved of Daniel Webster,
Uncle Charles Dunbar, who dozes while shaving,
chatty little sister Sophia, and John and Helen, who buzz in often
from their Roxbury and Taunton teaching jobs—
how can a few rowdy boys hurt?
Father will be hiding in the pencil-factory anyway.
A bell-clapper herself, Cynthia looks forward to more uproar
than the usual transients pounding the door.
But only four unsuspecting boys from Boston show up.

Then a mercy—venerable Concord Academy folds.
Thoreau rents the space dirt-cheap and snags the name for free:
CONCORD ACADEMY Six dollars per quarter Henry D. Thoreau, Instructor.
When enrollment soars—where else can the pupils go?—
the Thoreau brothers run the school together.
With a roll reading Bacon, Bartlett, Beath, Bigelow, Brooks, Burr,
Dakin, Gerrish, Hoar, Hosmer, Keyes, Kilham,
Lee, Loring, Rice, Tolman, Tuttle, Wood—

they still have room for more.
Louisa May Alcott, that galloping girl, arrives with her sister.
But best of all is the coming of
the beautiful Edmund Sewall of Scituate,
grandson of Mrs. Thoreau's star-boarder, Mrs. Colonel Joseph Ward.
Lucky band, the universe is their schoolhouse.

The Forerunner

I might have loved him, had I loved him less.
  –Henry David Thoreau

On June 17, 1839, the rumbly coach from Scituate
deposits eleven-year-old Edmund Sewall and his pretty mother
on the dusty planks along Main Street
that lead to the best boardinghouse in Concord.
Best, if you love hot buttery breads
and Mrs. Thoreau's savory but meatless meals.
That suits Mrs. Colonel Joseph Ward and Prudence very well.
Such fare is one of the country pleasures now in store
for her married daughter and her grandson Edmund—
sakes, how he's grown!
Like a June daybreak, the boy smiles for his grandmother,
then colts around Cynthia's parlor
until she calls Henry to entertain him for the week.

The job is far from hard.
Sailing on the Concord, they navigate in tandem,
the man hauling the oar,
the boy steadily unrolling the homemade sail.
Both are hungry for the mild June sun
and for sightings of minnows and watersnakes
swimming in the shade along the banks.
When they hike out to the Cliffs,
the boy controls his urge to sprint on ahead and is rewarded
when Thoreau gathers a charmed squirrel into the crook of his arm
and quietly calls him to come and see.
Loitering about Walden Pond,
the two often fall as silent as brothers, or lovers,
long past the need for speaking.
With awe in common, they watch
a heron's legs inscribe a watery trail in air.

After the Sewalls have gone,

Thoreau can't shake the effect of the boy's beauty.
He writes a few stilted quatrains,
praising the openness of this "gentle boy"
and blaming his own repression for being "taken unawares."
He encloses the poem with a letter to Edmund,
who reads it aloud to his family,
then cheerfully endures a ribbing from the Sewalls.

Ellen Sewall

Wampumpeag from spirals of
a channeled whelk,
her cheek evokes white violets.

Nothing prepares him for her beauty.
Aboriginal as a mollusk,
bones order flesh.

Brown-rose curve of closed lip,
deep-set eyes hinting
strength and native intelligence.

As her first hours in Concord pale,
he writes out
his utterly silent passion:

One green leaf shall be our screen,
Till the sun doth go to bed,
I the king and you the queen. . . .

Love awash in one fierce wave,
lower tides lure
her whorled shell to a wider sea.

I Can Not Tell You Half I Have Enjoyed Here

Ellen Sewall's letters glow.
She'd have folks back home in Scituate
believe Concord is on a plane
with Paradise.

Walking. To Fairhaven Bay. To Walden Pond.
Berrying. In the North Branch,
where the darkest, sweetest berries lie.
That pup Thoreau leading the way. She calls him—

Henry. And his brother—John. Fawning,
as if those Transcendental heathens were her own
brothers. So what if Henry musters cash to take her out
to ogle a cameleopard. Cheap carnival fraud.

Like him. Then, cheaper afternoons. Sailing downriver
while—just think of it—Aunt Prudence lazes
prudently aft. And just as prudently rides behind them
in that disgusting horse-cart he hires. Worse—

he has pressed his strong brown fingers
through her loosened hair, felt her naked skull
and read its bumps in the guise of a silly lark
at some ridiculous party. *Phrenology!* Pah! No doubt

a French charade invented by Thoreau
to touch and exult in her
"amativeness" and "philoprogenitiveness."
Poppycock. Yet, it pleases her.

No wonder she prevaricates:
I can not tell you half I have enjoyed here.
Between those lines, one can clearly read
the censored half, all too well. The brown hands

that parted her hair, the same hands that
lovingly cradled a bream in the pond.
Yet stupidly he claimed to have found no bumps at all.
According to that bunk, she's either a genius or an idiot.

The Reverend Edmund Q. Sewall
flicks away his daughter's carefully written page,
unaware that Thoreau has already confided to his journal:
There is no remedy for love but to love more.

John's Girl

For all the world, clearly—
it's plain as day—
John's got the inside track.

John invents the droll and merry
tales that make her
tinkly laughter ring for a week.

Caring for her health,
solemn Henry lectures her
against drinking coffee and tea.

When at last she must depart,
tearfully, assuaging opals follow her home,
a love-gift from John.

Henry sends a book—
the poems of Jones Very—
to her annoyed and incredulous father.

For all the world, she's John's girl.
But at her desk, it's Henry who compels her
affectionate pen to tweak his nose:

Does Dr. Thoreau continue
to give advice gratis?
I do not clean my brasses

half as quick
without the accompaniment
of his flute.

Stoic

That autumn he distracts
himself by writing
on the bitter satires of Persius.

Clusters of grapes wither;
lavish leaves yellow
and fall. He moves on

to work a stiff translation
of *Prometheus Bound*.
Obsessed by

an idea of bravery.
For him,
every mercy is strained.

Black powders of decay
wilt the gardens,
once galleries of perfume.

Talons of ice
scratch his windowpane,
leaning in at him.

Stark awake, he lies
pinned to his mattress
while a shaft drills

his heart. The woman
he loves loves his
brother. His closest comrade.

Whom he'll not betray
for all the fire
stolen by Prometheus.

June and All

Ellen Sewall, fragrant and bemused,
comes to him in June.
In the flesh, not in waking dream.

Summer afternoon, summer afternoon—
sauntering toward Walden.
On a weathered plank of the Red Bridge

he carves her name with H. D. T.
Hazed in gold and green,
he rows her across the steaming water.

Free and young and lovely,
she sits in the stern watching for bream
while he plies the oars.

Nothing but her form, a still-life spirit
haloed by sun,
comes between himself and the sky.

So might all their lives be—
picturesque—if free enough to part
the cloud-haze obscuring her with the horizon.

Scituate Beach

At Scituate the sea buffets marled rock,
exhausts itself and falls back
before gathering force for a fresh attempt.
Tidally so, John Thoreau courts Ellen Sewall,
foisting a visit on her folks at home.

Had he only known enough to stay away.
Irritation and anger cast a pall
as the Sewalls drown in mortification;
the Reverend Edmund Q. Sewall is enduring humiliations
of a public dismissal by his irked congregation.

Likewise, in the waters off Scituate,
a portly book-gilled horseshoe crab swims
awkwardly, upside down,
until a revolting tide sweeps it clean ashore,
where it lies, exposed to curiosity and rot.

Still, the beach at evening is lovely.
A place for lovers to escape after a cheerless meal,
with Aunt Prudence in tow.
Between land and sea, the contemplative sand
engraves their silence in runes.

When Prudence flops down,
they saunter beyond earshot with eyes lowered,
as if searching for seashells. Aware of scarce time,
John abruptly offers himself to Ellen.
She accepts him on the spot.

That night the sea throws itself ashore
with no more anguish than Ellen Sewall's confession
to her mother—she prefers John's brother.
Mrs. Sewall demands a break-up. Any Transcendental son-in-law
would complete her husband's disgrace.

Jilted overnight, John Thoreau sends Ellen
a single crystal for remembrance.
At his brother's rejection, Henry inhales a reckless freedom.
Confessing joy to an indigo sky, he writes:
Night is spangled with fresh stars.

Star-Crossed Letters

Landlocked in Watertown, New York,
Ellen Sewall endures an enforced removal from
the lovelorn Thoreaus as the last blush of autumn drains.
To abolish drear, she composes letters filled with
nostalgia for their past summer in Concord.

To her Aunt Prudence Ward, she emotes,
I always think of you when I see any beautiful prospect.
Then coyly adds, *You are not the only person
in Mrs. Thoreau's family whom such scenes call to mind. . . .
What great work is Henry engaged in now?*

Dated November 1st, as if in reply, Henry's proposal
arrives like a soul flown up from his journal.
*I thought that the sun of our love should have risen
as noiselessly as the sun out of the sea, and we sailors
have found ourselves steering between the tropics. . . .*

Sure enough of her to declare a mutual love,
he doesn't dream she'll show his letter.
Reverend E. Q. Sewall demands a point-blank refusal,
made in a "*short, explicit* and *cold* manner to Mr. T."
His daughter obeys, then confesses to her aunt:

*I never felt so badly at sending a letter in my life. . . .
It was such a pity. . . . Burn my last.*

The Husbandry Poet

With a new leveler he's surveying near the river
on that leafless eleventh day of November
when Ellen Sewall's letter is delivered into his hand.
The parched white square tells all.
Its brittle strokes stiffen in Thoreau's woolen pocket.
They silence his journal for weeks into winter.

On the first of December, can it matter that
Margaret Fuller of *The Dial* rejects
his much toiled-over essay, "The Service"?
Bluff, he'd once called it "A chapter on Bravery."
To a point of despair, it does matter. To the once-brave,
life is now an untilled, weed-ridden battlefield.

His balm is reading, reading, reading.
Reading nature as much as any page—a leaf, a wing,
a ripple, a reed. In postures of the forest he discerns
his own crumpling form—erect, humble, sneaking.
This plain sheet of snow which covers the ice of the pond
is not such a blancness as is unwritten, but such as is unread.

All colors are in white. The ink-furrowed pages of
Virgil's poem of the Earth that he plows through
mentally till his own battlefield with bland, Virgilian calm.
How to tell good soil from bad; how to bend an elm
into a plow handle; how to plow, weed, irrigate; how to make
a threshing floor; to tend vines and trees; to keep bees. . . .

Virgil's contented farmer works with his hands
in the same way that Virgil carefully labors to grow
his *Georgics* in praise of rural self-sufficiency.
Finally Thoreau gains a stoic strength to write:
It is great praise in the poet to have made husbandry famous.
Husband to none, he, too, will sow fertile sheets of snow.

Under the Cold Cold Moon

> *To sigh under the cold cold moon*
> *for a love unrequited,*
> *is to put a slight upon nature;*
> *the natural remedy would be to fall in love*
> *with the moon and the night,*
> *and find our love requited.*
> *—Henry David Thoreau*

Pierced by Ellen Sewall's rejection,
he reels in his rational mind
towards the winter moon's marble arms.

But the gibbous moon passes him
without notice. His bleating lamb of boyhood
stiffens and dies. Falling in love with

nature on the rebound torments him.
But also, his mother's boarder Lucy Jackson Brown,
whose *eyes are like the windows of nature.*

And too, Mary Russell, little Waldo's governess,
who inflames his journal: *Every maiden conceals a fairer flower*
and more luscious fruit than any calyx in the field.

Love under the cold cold moon requites
his humanity about as well as
love with a shrub oak, or a thicket of twigs.

Bush

So anti-slavery he rues paid servants, Emerson mulls
the stove-door's rude caw. Could he repair it?
If he chose, he might undertake to fell its firewood, too.
Gee and haw a pair of oxen through snow with logs
he'd saw and split himself, sweating their first heat.

Orchardist, gardener, pruner, propagator—
he could be those, too. If he chose. Germinator
of ideas, he was this already. Barring editorial bugs,
an intellectual broadcaster and planter. Much has he
thrilled to harvest-dreams beyond a self-sown thought.

But now, through his well-polished study-window,
his restless gaze falls upon the white discomfort
of an untoward April snow. Should he take Alcott's cue?
Turn his wife and their children into Brook Farmers?
The oxymoronic plan is for all to work so none will have to.

Can such pie-in-the-sky be trusted? Doubt shades across
the very question when he remembers Alcott's arbor.
Well, Hawthorne may slog about in the pig-manure if
that's what he believes in—the thought of that handsome face,
all a-muck with pig, elicits a craggy Brahmin grin.

No, there's a little green desk in that tiny room
just at the top of the stairs. Not much, but adequate
for a simple live-in man to write upon if he's content
to manage the household chores, half-time. Hands to work,
heart may roam, wherever. He will invite Thoreau.

The Children

He claims no redeeming trait
except loving the way
a wild thing cleaves to tilth or twig.

Lichens scaling rocks comprise
his ancient kin.
A white oak in the greenwood, his faith.

Surely green was the first hue
of his soul, he feels,
transforming a sunrise in the autumn hills.

The children of Concord adore him,
they are so close to earth
and heaven—their new eyes glisten with his.

Mimics Ellen and Edith, touched
by his voice, become his
reed pipes, birch whistles, rattling gourds.

Little Waldo kneels to a tuft of violets
he's shown him, kissing them
without plucking a one.

From his strong shoulders, the children survey
a pondful of stars. Sweet, blue
as the berries they eat with his stories.

Lidian

Those winter afternoons
when he comes in from long walking
in the wet or frozen woods,

he leaves his mud-sodden shoes
in the frigid shed
and steps into the kitchen,

never failing to blush
as he hastens
through this womanly domain.

It has no kind of resemblance
to the boudoir.
Yet he will colour.

In a hush, as is her way,
she will have to call him down
from the green desk

to keep them company
beside the fire, she will say,
but will not say

she knows his feet are cold.
Together, while the children play
like small bears on the rug,

they sit and talk of quiet things,
what he's seen,
where in the woods he's been.

Quiet woman, dark hair
smoothly tucked into white voile,
bride-like, innocent.

Yet, those infants at her feet,
her swelling lap.
Alone with her, housekeeping,

he dreams of her as that other one,
dark hair loosened,
all the sweet babies theirs.

The Budding Tree

For her gloves he has inset
beneath her chair a slender drawer
that rivals the shim of a poem.

He likes to think of her
unsheathed hands placing their
mask inside his carpentry.

He feels that she and he are one
with the sacrificial
maple tree, a prim and silent offering.

But for her child, that
little bud of being, Edith named, he hazards
language, if not metaphor.

Edith, he permits
to know him without impediment;
to play as no woman may.

Edith in bud
rid'st upon my shoulders as the sphere,
turning on me thy sage reserved eye. . . .

As for her sage and reserved mother,
well as she has always liked him,
he still grows upon her.

Eleven Days to Eternity

On the brisk first morning of the new year, a Saturday,
John Thoreau is stropping his razor
when it slips and cuts a sliver
from his left ring finger.
Shoving the skin back on, he applies a bandage
and pays it no more attention.
By mid-week, pain shoots through the finger.
Unwrapping it, he finds the head of skin *mortified*.
That evening he calls on Dr. Bartlett, who
dresses it and sends him home.
Shuddering through the dark and dense cold,
John feels acute pains with other strange sensations
telegraphing through his whole body.
He barely reaches the house and crawls into bed.
The next morning he awakens and tries to call out;
but an odd stiffness clamps his jaws shut.
That night violent spasms seize his body.
Frightened, his mother calls for a doctor from Boston,
post-haste.
Only to advise John that he must die.
Soon, and in great pain.

–Is there no hope?
–None.
–The cup that my Father gives me,
shall I not drink it?

By turns he passes through wild delirium
and cheerful composure.
Then, as if preparing for a brief journey,
he bids casual goodbyes to his stricken family.
At two o'clock on a Tuesday afternoon, January 11, 1842,
John Thoreau leaves a world of time
in his brother's arms.

Phantoms

As a small child, he found a fascination in the axe
his father used to split limbs of healthy oak and elm.

So alluring was its flash that his stealthy hands, so
dexterous, somehow failed. The blade cut off his toe.

That shock long forgotten, now from dawn to dusk
he stares through space. And the phantom sinew stirs.

To break his stupor, his two sisters lead him outside
without a coat. A startled crow drops a limbful of snow.

Ruffling their merino skirts, they slip back to the house.
Sophia coaxes him to sing now, as he once used to do.

With dull gray eyes, he only looks at her, and remains
as silent as a severed cord. Then, eleven days after

their brother John's death, he falls into violent delirium.
With all the same symptoms of John's fatal tetanus.

Called on the fly, the physician stands back, stymied.
Searching the patient's body has uncovered no wound.

It seems he will live. Must live, as if his brother were
still a present limb, and not a phantom pain of loss.

The coda of death drums on. Before January ends,
scarlatina claims little Waldo, the bright child he'd loved.

When *he* was small, he had not dreamed of final things.
Merely saw the flash while the beam split, like wings.

An Eagle Wrestling the Wind

Since the death of a Concord fixture—
sweet old Reverend Ezra Ripley,
who did not live to shepherd his lambs
young John Thoreau and little Waldo Emerson into everlasting life—
the Old Manse has been moldering for want of a human touch.
In the spring of 1842, Henry Thoreau is afflicted with
the same kind of moldering that affects the vacant manse.
Some days he stands for hours making pencils.
Others, he traipses through lackluster fields, meditating
on his own footprint and its dueling eternities, behind and ahead.
Often he mulls the glow of primeval energy warming the land
which spawned a now half-dead Indian race.

One blustery late-March day he walks up to the Cliffs.
Looking down, he spies two little hawks playing on the gusts.
Like butterflies they spiral in alternation, one above the other,
swooping from side to side in a basin of tree-tops,
as if swung by a pendulum. Above the bowl of trees, a shadow flits.
Glancing up, he starts at a violent rush of tremendous wings.
An eagle appears, wrestling the higher winds.
Time after time, it sails against the driven air, then falls back,
like a ship rocked onto her beam end. As if preparing
to catch a thunderbolt, its talons clutch at the diaphanous sky.
What a life the gods have granted—he feels its pang—
too strange for sorrow, too strange for joy.

From that March day,
as into the pathless depth of a Cretan labyrinth,
he feels himself floating into the radiant womb of Nature.

III.

*I must confess there is nothing so strange to me as my own body.
I love any other piece of nature, almost, better.*

–Henry David Thoreau

A Wedding Garden

The prospect of a bride in the Old Manse
gently rouses Concord from its stoic
mourning of the coffined past. A bride
in all her loveliness of being in love, will grace
the vacant house on her first day as a wife.
In the moldering shade of the pastor's room
her bridegroom will entreat her
with variations on songs of Solomon.
On the Musketaquid pale ice floes swim
into torrents swollen with spring rain,
and Walden Pond lies glassily under the sun.

With the scent of waking earth and trees
in his nostrils, Thoreau collects rake and plow
and barrows them to the neglected ground
of the dead pastor who'd christened him.
For a moment he surveys the tangled patch
of broken mullein and wasted morning glories.
As winter's blast flags like a blackened vine,
he braces the plow against the thawing soil,
holds it down hard, and heaves forward.
When Hawthorne and his bride Sophia arrive
home on their wedding day, July 8, 1842,

they discover Thoreau has planted their garden
with a husbandry worth ten of any in Eden.

Beauty and the Beast

> *Mr. Thorow dined with us yesterday. . . . He is as ugly as sin, long-nosed, queer-mouthed, and with uncouth and somewhat rustic, although courteous manners. . . . But his ugliness is of an honest and agreeable fashion, and becomes him much better than beauty.*
>
> *—Nathaniel Hawthorne*

At a touch, Hawthorne's Swiss music box
tosses a grist of melodic coins into the air
from its milling cogs and wheels of brass.

A charm of art and craft, it bewitches even
the reticent Mr. Thoreau who, uninvited, sits
in the Old Manse parlor like a Sunday child,

absorbing a tune unwinding from the works.
Wondering how he, or anything, could live again,
he'd planted their wedding garden in the spring.

Either springtime or his own hand scattered
fertility over the patch; for now its yield forces
Sophia Hawthorne to invite him in to dine,

reluctantly. At table, her young bridegroom,
so handsome that pedestrians often stop
and stare, mentally compares Thoreau to sin.

Afterwards, Thoreau invites his host for a spin
on the river in his handmade boat, *Musketiquid*.
It obeys its steersman so well that, full of envy,

Hawthorne offers seven dollars on the spot
to purchase this apparently flawless craft.
But in Hawthorne's hands, the boat turns ugly—

bewitched! It aims towards every compass-point
except the one he wants. But when Thoreau
takes the oar again, to Hawthorne's chagrin,

the *Musketiquid* calms like a beautiful trained steed.

Winterfire 1842

Frigid pine boards protest his step
until he pauses beside his small green desk
to look beyond the pallorous window,
where stalactites of ice emulate prison bars.
In the dooryard below, wizened lilacs scrape clapboards.
Capes and gowns engage in a ghoulish white dance.
Barely awake, he wonders if nature has conceived of
this strange new design for burnt-out artists.

Gradually the normal sounds of life revive—
the sore-throat crowing of a bilious cock;
the repetitive barking of a tethered, unfed dog;
the achey hatcheting of poplar for kindling;
the stirring of cattle inside the stock-barns,
their anxious bawling for grain or hay.
He can just make out a dour twilight sunrise,
now searing the froth with a slender foil.

Unlatching the pantry door, he quickly inhales
the sharp cold sting of the firmament.
Spectral and still, the myopic morning
still claims a fey disguise of Tartarian dusk.
As drifts fill his boots, he wades to the woods' edge.
Razor-close, a shaft of pine crashes. Blood rushes
to his face with a thrill of near-disaster. He feels,
burning in nature, a subterranean fire no cold can chill.

A Leaf in Ice

> *A diseased bundle of nerves standing between time and eternity like a withered leaf.*
> —Henry David Thoreau

Lackluster
book of pages,
himself at twenty-five.

Love sick,
fear and ire divide
his mind like

a pendulum
between vitality and
chronic illness.

Chthonic
leaf: the look of life,
bogged in ice.

The white house
on Lexington Road,
a clapboard trap.

Poet-in-residence—
In reality,
unpaid chore-boy.

Bravado, all his
paeans to bravery,
now curdled in rejections.

Like the leaf,
crimson with shame,
lodged in ice.

He *must* go.
Emerson, ensconced
on Staten Island, must tend

his own wife.
Thor—Thoreau—must
sail to New York.

Snuggery Blues

Crux of his career, tutor in New York!
But the smug brown house on Staten Island proves
unsnug to the unsung hero of his own life.
He feels like a penniless governess in her garret
at the Snuggery. The whole house, a drab anemia
of spirit, papered over with ghastly floral debris.
In the foyer, calling cards lie like scat on a silver tray.
The *Annual* maps a catty-corner of dust
beside a gaunt sansevieria with snake-hung leaves.
The vaporous parlor, whaleboned with folding doors,
holds its breath for visitors. A faded whelk,
or two, rest like chunks of chalk on the mantle.
If oceans of the Southern Cross flail and toss within,
they roar unheard by their owner's ears.

Even the pale Snuggery children,
rousted from doldrums, cry with shallow voices.
Weak sobs skim their little hearts,
fearful of much sound, but drowning in dullness.
Still, the Snuggery houses a highly respectable family.
The tutor observes rounds of social routine
while the tall clock pounds his brain with its chimes.
A sense of waste erodes him. Worse than a dune on the Cape.
He longs for crochety Concord as he stares
at the burgundy-green wallpaper trimmed with black oak.
Sallying forth—what travesty—into this moneyed desert.
He recalls his awe at seeing a lone tulip tree, crowned in gold.
Now by a ship-clogged harbor, he mourns all
the once-strong horses and oxen, carcasses washing ashore.

Thoreau in New York

Pee-stench clouds
so many doorways and alleys
that the rank flood of human waste

threatens to break
the frayed and ravaged thread
clinging to the hem of

privilege and wealth
which propel business moguls
and society clans

past the ache of starved bones
beaten dead
in rotten traces.

The pigs in the street are
      the most respectable part
of the population.

Dear Lidian—

His letters confirm the words
he's not had power
to speak to her, even in the hush at day's end.

Elevating her as some elder sister,
or lunar influence,
he measures the light of sister moon

and thinks he discerns her coming,
blue-lit
from cold heaven, her dark image

traced upon a sphere of light.
His thought, her attendant evening star. . . .
But in the course

of composing, he grows as practical
as a seducer
playing the generous cavalier:

*I, perhaps, am more willing
to deceive by appearances than you say you are. . . .*
He fails to imagine

his mother's badgering her
to hand over his letters, then snorting:
O yes, Henry is very tolerant.

The Linen and Woolen Man

> *I hold together remarkably well as yet,*
> *speaking of my outward linen and woolen man. . . .*
> *   –Henry David Thoreau*

On the first of October, 1843, a day of mists and fruitfulness—
in Concord, the purpled grapes—he writes his mother

a rueful confession. He's found no Eldorado in New York.
My bait will not tempt the rats–they are too well fed.

If he could bow to write something companionable,
the *Ladies' Companion* would pay. But stooping is not his way.

His way is a translation of the Nature he expects to be immanent
everywhere, transcending dross. But here, the street-pulse

churns out human aspirants: Roaming the streets,
Norwegians with—God's truth—strapped-on axes and pitchforks.

Pasty English operatives, swindling back their birthrights.
Rough red Irish, cooking their crude dinners on the pavement.

Orientals, swathed in all the robes and turbans they possess.
Perhaps one of them will be dubbed Count of Wisconsin.

It must be very bad for children to see so many humans at once,
he worries. Like unearthing a ball of snakes in spring.

One First Day, at the Hester Street Friends Meeting, Lucretia Mott
rises and rails against slavery. A brief, sickly ray of hope.

Reading his letter aloud, Cynthia Thoreau gusts on: *I don't know*
when I shall be home; I like to keep that feast in store.

Among the Ruins

Vicious wild dogs roam
the littered shore at Sandy Hook,
where he sits among the stones of a ruin
to watch the sea widen into sky.
Far off ships could be
sea-salmon, plunging towards
some deep ancestral spawning place.
He, too, might find his way,
riding the waves on such a ship.

Then a day comes when
he snatches a mauled and crying pup
from the jaws of the pack.
At once it is clear
that he must take himself back
to the rivers and ponds of Concord.
Where rainwater sheets the fields,
revealing an azure glimpse of heaven.
And where he wades naked into Walden.

Making Pencils, Thoreau Discovers the Secret of Success

After the New York debacle,
the house in Concord
looks more than good.

To pay off debts,
he reinvents the pencil
for Thoreau & Co.

Plumbago and Bavarian clay.
Mix and bake.
Rods hard as the devil.

Drill cedar cylinders.
Ram the rods in.
No split halves, no black paste.

By summer 1844, the pencil
is sold "expressly for
Artists and Connoisseurs."

His secret—simplicity.
The more clay,
the harder the instrument.

That Terrible Thoreau

For a normally damp New England April,
the deep subsoil remains uncommonly dry.
Vague and listless, drab fields and woods lie
exposed to the sky after thin snows dissolve.
A walker through last season's coarsened weeds
might recoil at hearing their achy complaint—
as if some ancient and rheumatic escapee
from the poor-farm had been trampled on.
Still, two trippers come exalting nature's glory.
Bare and silent, the woods signal a reproof.

A scruffy man of twenty-six looks the more
guilty part—larking at midday with a callow
Harvard student majoring in fecklessness.
This morning Henry Thoreau had paddled
Ed Hoar a mile up the low Sudbury River
to catch a scant nooning's mess of perch.
By the woods of Fair Haven, they hop out,
search pockets, then sponge a match from
a passer. Their campfire blackens the fish,
fast-breaks free, then bursts up like a rocket.

Slapping and stomping, beating the flames
with a rotten board—nothing stops the blaze.
The wildfire speeds away through the parch.
Panicking, Ed Hoar jumps into Thoreau's boat
and rows off. Thoreau sprints to a clearing
where a man listens to his alarm, then shrugs.
None of *his* stuff. Hoarse-voiced and gasping,
Thoreau finds the owner, who comes out to see.
By now a half-mile firestorm leaps limb to limb.
Without a word, Thoreau turns and walks away.

Atop the barren Fair Haven Cliffs, he finally
dares to watch the holocaust of screaming trees.

All his life he'll endure the tag *woods burner* spat
behind his back, which will ramrod even more.
Six years later he will claim against logic that
since trees can't be owned, no crime occurred
in his careless instigation of a *glorious spectacle!*
Sixty years later the old Wheeler girl will snap,
"Don't talk to me about Henry Thoreau"—
That terrible Thoreau! That terrible Thoreau!

Clapper and Bell

Colossal stiff-bonneted ants rallying for battle,
the abolitionist women of fourteen towns
swarm over the Concord Courthouse lawn.
After a heavy cloudburst, their best boots sink in mud;
but the women are impervious to daggled skirts and boots.
Fuming, they implore the sexton to ring the bell of warning
that a special town-meeting has been called. But
the impertinent man turns them down flat—even the doughty
Mrs. Joseph Ward and Prudence, and the sisters Thoreau.
Not by any political female will this sexton be swayed.

Her bonnet-bows askew, Mrs. Cynthia Thoreau
pins down every selectman she can find in the crowd:
Will not anyone force the sexton to do his duty? she shouts.
With a custard of diplomacy, she had persuaded
Mr. Ralph Waldo Emerson to come out today—
at long last—against slavery in America.
Now, to think that the great man's speech may held in limbo
by a mean-spirited stubborn sexton!
The humiliation of poor Mr. Emerson, waiting
to commemorate the *tenth anniversary* of emancipation
for all black people in the British West Indies—
waiting to pledge his support for the noble cause!
Now, with arms akimbo, he looks on a half-empty hall
because that ridiculous sexton holds no brief for abolition!
Gandering up and down, selectmen on the lam
duck past thick waves of crinoline.
One stage-whispers the stale joke about Mrs. Thoreau's tongue,
how it goes like a bell-clapper.

On this day, the first of August 1844, her son,
that terrible Henry Thoreau, *woods-burner*,
ambles downtown with that awful Ellery Channing, *skirt-chaser*.
Passing the dripping elms on Main Street,
they encounter a boiling-over in Concord

that contrasts sharply with their cool Catskills idyll.
Thoreau dumps his pack and heads straight for the action.
At the First Parish Church beside the Courthouse,
the sexton is making a show of snubbing the angry ladies.
Unnoticed, Thoreau slips into the church,
grabs the bell-rope with both hands and hauls down hard,
whooping like a Mohawk on the warpath.
The old iron bell thunders across the yellow fields
to those who have ears to hear and to those who don't, alike.

On Being Called a Sponge

Muttered scorn, the word wobbles in air
like the silken parachute of a seed

blown aloft from fields of dandelions.
He can hardly believe himself how it

yellows green, whitens blue, then with
a vengeance sinks a whorl of teeth in mud

stirred up from stables and parlors alike.
What's clearly meant to sow offense and hurt

strikes target. Thoreau's stung ear works so well
that rowdy dark hairs quill his neck;

and he vows to sheathe it in paid receipts.
For every last hill of beans he's purchased.

For room and board, marked *Paid* by his father.
Not a red cent will he owe—to anyone.

The House on Texas Street

Due west of the Fitchburg Railroad Station,
where the old Heywood farm maundered
in neglect through its comatose last illness,

Concord has laid out the new Texas Street.
Along with a locomotive whoop and a whistle,
staid Concordians might have yelled, "Yee-Haw!"

for all the uproar about lots going up for sale.
Thrilled long-distance down to her toes,
Mrs. Cynthia Thoreau waits on no ceremony.

Her long stride stretches into a gallop
toward the burdock fields of Texas Street.
Prickly as a rampant thistle, she stakes a lot.

Paces it out herself and cairns each corner.
Draws up a blueprint, hires her own carpenter.
Then informs her husband, guessing rightly

that he'll fork over the twenty-five dollars for
less than an acre. It's September in 1844,
reply is useless, and Tuttle will loan the lumber.

Already Henry is out there, swinging a pick
and a shovel, gouging out the cellar-hole.
Heaping aside the rubble, stoning it precisely.

All's well until the carpenter forgets a staircase.
Father and son lock eyes. Why'd she hire him
in the first place? They hammer out a plan.

In the end, the Thoreau house on Texas Street
looks like a two-story box. Left on a dump.
But Cynthia brags to any wretch she can collar.

Ashamed of scarring the ghostly Heywood fields,
her son plants apples, grapes, lilacs. All told,
some forty trees to disguise the place as home.

Concord Spring 1845

As sweet a mystery
as ever was,
what this world is
in spring bud.

Awakening woods
and glazed river,
songs of mating birds
and swelling waters.

The oven-bird thrums
his sawyer's strain.
The chewink upturns
volumes of dross.

Plethora of urges,
intoxication of scents,
spice of buried mint,
bark-bruise of birch.

Heartleap, heartleap—
the ache of the hickory's
sallow young leaves,
the white oak's sage fuse.

Bold life, the hymn
of change,
surges through his
quivering spirit,

as he enters the woods
strung with pearls
of pendant rain
on its rose-nippled buds.

Directive

Stacked on a wagon with horsehair sofa, parlor chairs,
walnut dining table, bureaus and chiffoniers,
bedsteads, linens, flatirons, kettles, and toasting forks,
Mrs. Thoreau's circus moves to the Texas Street house.

Chatter of grey squirrels and squawk of thieving magpies
competing for a sidewise dominion of house-noise
may well be slandered with disgust. Also, the chirping flock
of lady-boarders. But on Mother and Sophia, he's mum.

He cannot and will not hate women—he's susceptible.
It's blather he hates. What prevents his writing his book.
He cuts up his journal then rearranges the pages on
the Concord and Merrimack boat-trip with his brother.

What else can he do? His head feels like a bird's nest.
Twigged, leaved, twined, and muddled in a thatch.
Just in time, Channing's advice saves him from bedlam:
Get out. Retreat. Build a hut by Walden. Devour yourself alive.

The Pines of Walden

Arrowy pines, striplings,
shift tensions
in the late March wind,

betraying held breath.
They might have been
a lithe forest of

Tahatawan's warriors
waiting for the intruder
to pass on.

Vanished with his
young dreams,
that vision hides now

in bear-claw limbs
gouging needled loam
while his gleaming axe

chops them to death.
In his fragrant house,
arrowy ghosts will dance.

To Those Who Are Not Ashamed of Economy

On his mother's pantry shelf, Mrs. Lydia Child's
American Frugal Housewife presides, talking sense

TO THOSE WHO ARE NOT ASHAMED OF ECONOMY.
How much has he consulted her on the sly?

With his own eyes he's oftener than not seen
frugal wives proof a yeast to learn if it's alive.

Himself, in just two hours flat he shoveled out
a cellar hole, seven feet deep by six feet square.

Cut and hewed young pines for main and floor.
Framed a house to hold a cot, a table, and a chair.

Got the best thinkers in the country to come out—
Emerson, Alcott, Hawthorne—and raise the forms.

But every mortise and tenon came from good
live yeast: his own deft hand, his own clear mind.

If the house rose on a sponge, as some call him,
it stands proof of his life lived, volume after volume.

A Little Rumor like Salt

What's he *doing* out there?
You'd think he'd get lonesome with nobody to talk to.
It's ag'in nature, a man all by hisself.
Up to who knows what mischief.
Praps he'll set Mr. Emerson's woods afire, too.
What 'ud you do with the scallywag if you were his ma?
Not bake them pies and doughnuts
Sophia and her trot out to the pond ev'ry Satiddy.
Well—otherwise he'd starve to deef.
They say he sneaks in home to raid the cookie jar
every chanst he gets. Ornery pup.
But you know Cynthia. She'd rather die or kill
than hear a word ag'in her son.
Yup, you must button your lip to hear her brag
about his grand ee-conomy sper'ment. Lord knows,
Mrs. Lydier Child said ev'rythin there's to say 'bout that
in *The Frugal Housewife*. Prob'ly read it, durn 'is hide.
Plain sense for a woman. Pure genius, spouted off by a man!
Sojourners in nature—pah, an't we all!
Cook for oursel'es, too!
Har-rumph!
[Voices lower.]
They say ev'ry time Lidian Emerson rings her dinner bell
he bounds through the woods and over the fences
to be first at the dinner table.
Yup, and jest you knock on Alcott's door, and there he'll be
with his knees under the table.
Poor Abba, she got it hard enough puttin' up with
that penniless windbag of a husband.
Transcendental wild oats—what her own darter calls it.
Sartain, Concord men are on their way to hell in a handbasket.
'Stead of playin' Injun, that Thorow orter get married.
A woman 'ud set 'im straight.
Who could stand 'im?

Thoreau's Umbrella

Rain, a cherishing.
From time to time slate
holds its burst.

Time and again, relents,
letting cold April
pour through the woods.

Tensed, then loosening,
drops break
clean from cloud.

The pond's slick slope
eases, paths
wrinkle into rivulets.

The first spring rain
loiters upon
a seine of trees.

He loves this place,
flow drumming
every cell.

Thut! Thut! Thut!
Myriads upon
myriads—the Real—

In the womb of spring,
he inhales its wet
scent on his umbrella.

IV.

*I was always conscious of sounds in nature which my ears could never hear,–
that I caught but the prelude to a strain.*

–Henry David Thoreau

Starting for Conantum

Rowing downriver towards a place he calls Conantum,
he observes the moist and muggy air—
true April in New England—
and the enormous gray sheet hung across the west.
Still he plies the oar until drops fall,
counting on the wind to push him back to the launch.

The rain comes crashing in a rush.
Soaked already, he pulls the boat around and lifts the sail.
At once it is shot with driven rain.
Holding onto his umbrella in the stern,
he struggles to steady its flimsy dome over his head
while steering the oar homeward.

For a few moments, big drops pepper the water, wide apart.
Not the hard bullets of rain on a roof,
but a softer, liquid plashing
creating a kind of watercolor of double wateriness.
At the bridges he makes haste to lower the sail.
But at one stone arch, he loses track of his umbrella.

It swipes past him, dangling from the mast like a black wing.
Pawn to the erratic moods of the storm,
he is struck by the changing surfaces of the water,
now a pied tumult of traveling reflections.
Streams of light stretch between streams of dark,
as if different waters, loath to mingle.

Yet all dimple equally under the force of rain.
He makes a mental note, for writing out later. Nature loves
variety for its own sake. Here is April's genius—
raining with perfect ease from an infinite pool.
On the way home, he finds a swathe of green flame
in the ditches overflowing either side of the road.

Surveyor

By sheer chance he finds
the spirit-level on an axis.
With theodolite and tripod,
divider and sheaf of paper,
he trades new know-how
for cold, hardboiled cash.
Still how sweet to be paid
for doing a thing he loves:

Wandering fields and woods
in all weathers, fair or foul.
Challenging all phenomena
that meet his ready eye.
Through a telescopic lens
he travels planes and plots.
Then he realizes his error in
plotting the woods for woodlots.

Walking in Rainlight, Thoreau Considers His Eye

Transparent
lamp of the body,
this eye

lights a dark
tearful valley within
while pied

nature tints its
spectrum with liquid
optics of joy.

Birdland

An abode without birds is
meat without seasoning,
he has read in a French
translation of the Harivansa.

No such abode is his
Walden hut, but a simple
man-cage peered into by
wild birds of the woods.

Veery, tanager, wood-thrush,
field-sparrow, whippoorwill—
all fly to serenade him,
the cherished pet they keep.

An Arch over the Darker Gulf

All through a brain-burning northern summer,
Homer's *Iliad* lies on Thoreau's table.
Like the blood-orange locks of Achilles,
its pages curl in the damp heat.
Now and then, Thoreau reads a few lines of Greek;
but hoe-work and house-work compel him.

Still the linen touch of words racing
across fulvous fields like athletes in the funeral games
intoxicate his brain. Among Myrmidon bean-rows,
he wields his hoe, a pastoral sword of quest or conquest,
while his thoughts race the advancing hour of noon.
Hand or mind, competition rages under the sun.

Among yellow-eyes, he sees the girl Briseis, prodded
like a white heifer to Agamemnon's tent. Her fair brow
bowed like a wet leaf. Sent for, demanded
by the great king himself. Delivered on the word
of Achilles himself, his heart as bruised as hoed weeds.
Proud, he embraces her loss with bitter tears.

Through green-knit rows, up rises immortal Thetis,
alert to the cry of her son. From mistling foam,
he hears the gentle breathing of his name.
My dear child in tears? What troubles you?
Don't keep hurts inside–. Ashamed, he turns aside
his face and cries, *You know, you know*.

Exposing roots to the sun, Thoreau
pauses at the dismal intuition of the mother
who laments birthing a child with a double doom.
It's bad that he'll suffer a short life, but worse
that he must be pierced by heartbreak.
More knowledge than a goddess should bear.

Harder for Achilles himself is the death of his brother
in arms. The sight of Patroclus staggering under
the weight of Hector's spear clean through,
bowels to back, drives him insane with grief.
At noon the beanfield blazes with mirage.
The angry hoe hacks a red-gold lock off the sun.

From a Granite Ledge on Greylock, Thoreau Considers the Railroad

Life could be a count
of ties under steel rails

running down a page.
Roundhouse dispatched

to a terminal mound.
Railroad time means

no stops except at
appointed intervals.

Unload hogsheads of
brandy and molasses at

Cuttingsville, Vermont.
Bear bleats and bawls

from a thousand hills
into one barren yard.

Arrow an enormous
white pine over snowed-

in Green Mountains to
stick a main-mast onto

a New Bedford whaler.
But each tie pins a soul

under locomotive lines.

Loafing

From daybreak to noon or more, he idles
in the door-square of sun
allotted him by white and pitch pines, hickories, sumacs.
Wanders all over, going nowhere, in a reverie
while bird-racket above bursts wide open and vanishes,
descends on an arc or so, and on a notion,
darts noiselessly through his house.

Sometimes the chorus ebbs to a single voice
warbling an adolescent love song
or an *aria* sublime as a star on the brink of fall.
Among the thorny blackberries arching over the ground
he marks heaps of cones and burrs. Still the wild strawberries grow
between the sand cherries and the groundnuts.
Where johnswort and life-everlasting mass, an ovenbird calls.

A screech owl injects her threnody,
her *u-lu-lu* of regret and despair, mourning in sackcloth,
Oh-o-o-o-o that I never had been bor-r-r-r-n!
Even so, he rejoices in the dismal owl, and the sailing hawk,
and the tronking bullfrogs clad in muck. He loves
the lowing of a lonesome cow, the baying of dogs in disgrace.
Unrepentant wassailers along with him.

Solitude

Shirtsleeves rolled, he ambles to the pond's edge,
imbibing liquors of a calm evening.
His blunt choice to drink in the nights alone
somehow sullies sweet women and rude men
who take offense at his eccentric way.
Still it is his delicious evening;
he feels a wine-bibber with the poplars.
The same air that moves them ripples the pond
and raises the thick pelts on his bare arms.
Alert now, nocturnal woodlands invite
him with a correspondent unrepose
as he enters their dampening dark fold.
Once asked if the woods were lonely, he'd said,
Is not our planet in the Milky Way?

Therien/Thoreau

Axe and tin pail of woodchuck meat
stowed in a pitch pine, Therien
slips up behind Thoreau's retreat.
Fires off a shot.

Frenchman's laughter sets
the poplars all quaking and flickering
at a philosopher
blown clean off his pumpkin.

Ah, Therien, how droll.
Mais tres magnifique! Your friend
Thoreau seems your twin,
your harmonic counterpoint.

Your brawn carries the melody,
your rough woodchopper's
rhythm of the blood.
Animal/Anima—the pair of you.

Childlike, you listen to
Thoreau read his loved *Iliad*
to awe you. You stun him
with simple truth: *"That's good."*

Scholars unweave a rainbow
to discover this is so.
But for you, Therien—thought is
an axe swung hard but true.

Ah, Therien, how could you
pilfer his book
and leave him—for once—
disarmed by wonder?

Sophia's Sleep

Fragile as a bone cup,
the summer night spills prim
translucent starlight.

Oolong sipped,
head downed in goose,
Sophia fails to sleep.

It's her brother's first night
in the hut, alone
by that wilderness pond.

What gnaws and slithers on
his roof? What eye-tooth gleams
behind what pitch tree?

Hours drag a bloody moon
across a pool of gulping frogs,
dark and cruel and slow.

Sophia cannot sleep.
Virginal and clean, her gown
of muslin twists and creeps.

No avail. She must rise up
and raise her arsenal of dough.
At dawn hot loaves invade.

The Flute on the Pond

Resting his oars away from the shore,
he picks up a flute and plays
in harmony with the chanting birds.
The invisible chorale persists with
no hint of dissonance.

On the pond, mute shadows of leaves
shift to trembling reflections,
the way his breath tides across the flute
mimicking the airy compulsions
that blend him with Walden.

In his minimal house, an alert mouse
skims an open book. Beads an eye.
Pricks an ear. Sprigs a tail. Is gone.
The pond-music flows on. Until
winds shift, and he lays the flute down.

Who Will Pay the Ferryman?

The black man left at Thoreau's shack
gives off the sick smell of cold fear

increased by the dark night drenching
such human transactions.

Into a moist palm Thoreau presses
a hunk of bread and a sack of small coins.

Then the two dissolve through
blind thickets Thoreau knows by heart.

Many a night he's found his way
through Walden Woods in such ink.

In town streets, lit lamps of kerosene
threaten to expose the skulkers

slipping from shade to shade, even past
Sam Staples thinking in his privy.

Mrs. Thoreau's safe-house looms high
above its stark young shrubs.

Past her door, into her woodwork,
the black man fades toward the North Star.

Walden Sky Water

October afternoon,
Every leaf and stone,
web and twig
shines as when clad in the dew
of a spring dawn.

The pond set in woods
has turned into a mirror
framed with reflective gems.
He sees himself in
gray pearls and blue jade.

Fingerling perch well up,
dimpling the water.
Birds bronze in sunlight,
wheeling and hovering,
fluid and transparent.

A dustcloth of cloud
wipes more light
across the liquid mirror.
Ultramarine springs up
at once from quicksilver

as if his blinded eye
has entered into
all nature, transcended
the watery sky,
been refracted in crystal.

Confessions of a Nineteenth-Century Naturalist

How low he falls
to drink a cup of coffee.
But to please his mother,
he dashes a morning's hopes.

How low he falls
to sip a dish of tepid tea.
But to placate his maiden aunts,
he dashes a simpler nooning.

No one can laugh him
out of the notion that clattering cups
corrupt human nature as much
as an opium-eater's narghileh.

If he lies, looking into a river-flow
or a transparent pool,
a draught of clarity braces him
unlike any sensual trough.

Puritan Romantic! How he falls
to lure and wrench
a rainbow trout from its native rill
only to founder in his gut.

In time the muskiness of flesh
revolts his tongue.
Dead meat, fat-streaming corpse.
A rot in his throat.

He spells it out in a book:
Our whole life is startlingly moral–
and given to narcoleptic sleep,
when the snake glides from its hole.

The View from the Taffrail

Leaving Tours to embark
on a ship crossing the gray-salt Atlantic,
Jean Thoreau doesn't give a hoot

for himself as someone's
first ancestor to set an undersized Gallic
foot into the New World.

Windless hours on end,
when the sullen ocean drones, he kills time
watching impressed boys picking oakum

from heaps of rotten hemp.
He sees them tar the chosen threads
and caulk the leaks in a ship made of trees.

Does smallish Jean Thoreau
connect the caulking of a vessel bound to fail
with the voyage of life itself?

His unimagined descendant will sail,
self-taught, through a carpentry of youthful boats
called *Rover* and *Red Jacket*.

Doing low oakum-work for himself,
this late Thoreau leans far
beyond the taffrail of an even greater craft

to search the wake that follows.
From the taffrail, he revels in the view
of unfamilial streams widening behind his ship.

A Funny Thing Happens on the Way to the Cobbler's Shop

Hay cut, peas done, rhubarb gone to puff,
beans in puny leaf, potatoes eaten with the peas—
what is there to do on a fly-bitten July evening
but badger the village misfit, young Thoreau?

Grumbling in his gut, constable Sam Staples, also
jailer and tax collector, thinks so. But if Henry
had not appeared, boots in hand, showing off
that Indian gait of his, he'd *not* have thought so.

Head-scratch. Ahh. Poll tax. Years in arrears
by Henry D. Thoreau. A lazy fact of Concord life,
something to do with some stiff-backed principle
now shoved under a hazy stack in Sam's mind.

"Henry, if you don't pay, I shall have to lock you up
pretty soon." Sam yawns, chewing the affable fat.
"As well now as any time, Sam." Rats of botheration.
A chore he'd not planned. "Well, come along then."

Late that night, a prisoner in a nearby cell begins
a litany of howls: "What is life? So this is life!"
Thoreau sticks his head against the bars and yells,
"Well, what *is* life, then?" Silence. Ruckus quelled.

Sam Staples no sooner gets home, sheds his boots,
and cozies to the fire than his daughter flies at him.
A black-veiled lady at the back door has thrust in
a wad of bills—to exonerate poor Henry Thoreau!

Sam chuffs. Durned if he'll lug his boots back on.
That pestiferous "poet" can stew the night in jail.
In the morning, when Sam tries to kick him out,
Henry is as mad as the devil. Huffs, he won't go!

Claims his meddling aunt Maria poked in her nose.
Scuttled his vow to pay not a red cent to condone
those defenders of slavery in the Statehouse. Wisely,
Emerson chides: "The state is an old cow—*feed her*."

The Picnic Grove

Summer afternoon in Concord village
evokes the same-old miseries—female yards of skirts
bustled out in sunbursts of nankeen.

Sleeves puffed up to rival ripe muskmelons.
Brain-clutching bonnet-helmets.
Summer afternoon, summer afternoon,

a moaning fluid constricted in female misery.
Why not abscond to the pine-groves
of Walden, to picnic for some cause or other

on Thoreau's cooling doorstep?
Boiling abolitionists steam up sumptuous plans
to mark the freeing of West Indian slaves.

While righteous women lay out
the baked meats, scholarly men such as
Emerson, W. H. Channing, and Reverend Caleb Stetson

orate on the stern beauties of conscience.
So difficult in July, what with heated ideals vying with
a lowdown hunger for huckleberry pie.

Awarded just desserts, eminent men and hot women
dissolve to swattings on a dusky path.
Thoreau's wandering feet turn to wilder groves.

Ktaadn

     1.

From the beginning the mountain spotted them:
     their buggy crawling from Bangor towards Mattawamkeag,
creaking to a halt in Indian villages to watch
     the long bateaux bent and laced by deft brown hands,
or to hire on a native guide who gets drunk and fails to show.
     Greenleaf's latest map of Maine—the mountain must have laughed—
a labyrinth of errors but cleverly traced onto an oiled paper
     by that Concord man, Thoreau.
When the boaters spring up the rapids of the Millinocket, plying

twelve-foot poles, their bateau grazes rocks like a salmon.
     The mountain half-expects a deadly spawn, and hopes for it.
Not in the cards. The wiry man from the flats carries on
     with excited shouts about a thing he calls Symplegades.
Austerely noting a challenge, the mountain frowns,
     throwing an immense cascade of shadows across its face.
The chilled men shiver, but remain determined to pitch
     a flimsy cotton-cloth tent north of North Twin Lake.
Spitefully the mountain hires a wind to fan sparks from their fire

onto the tent, which swirls like a bridal veil, then collapses in smudge.
     A droll pleasure fills the mountain at the sight of them
scrambling to drag the bateau into the woods and prop up one side
     enough to cover their heads with feet stuck towards the fire.
Salmon strung out to dry for pemmican look not half so absurd.
     For a few hours the mountain, wrapped in a high dudgeon, dozes.
But through a fog after dawn, it becomes aware of the bateau
     being poled, rowed, portaged across lakes, streams, and carries.
Then the interlopers reach Sowadnehunk Deadwater—only twelve miles

away from the mountain's summit. For the first time, it feels a stab
     of compunction, realizing it must trouble itself to gird
for the inevitable foolishness of inept climbers, followed by

        the even more wearisome intrusions of hallooing rescuers
with ridiculous hound dogs sniffing and baying for nought.
        The mountain prepares to cashier the mangled bodies and bones
which even the catamount may never gnaw. Weariness and prudence
        stop the men for the time being. But morning finds them
swinging provisions and gear into the tops of saplings to foil the bears.

    2.

All day long they climb, placing one boot above the other, until
        repetition seems about to destroy their minds. Then
at four o'clock, they make a scraggly camp in view of the summit.
        That would be that, giving the mountain welcome respite to devise
what next would befall the expedition. But the confounded man
        from the flats climbs on alone, leaving the rest to the mundane
chores of making camp and nursing blisters and bruised shins. Who dares
        come on alone, pulling himself up beside booming vertical falls
fifteen to thirty feet wide, clutching the roots of birches and firs?

Then, tramping on a level rod or two before climbing the next falls?
        As he advances, the torrents never diminish in breadth
but roar down onto and among massive rocks, as though tossed
        violently out from the very clouds. Surely this man crawls
onto Satan's own chair in Chaos, so arduous is the climb to
        the nearest, though not the highest, peak. Like a child
he scrambles on all fours atop black spruce-trees, old as the flood,
        but merely ten or twelve feet tall, their flat foliage
blue and blunted by centuries of resistence to the bleak, solid cold.

He pads for rods across the crowns of the spruces, so overgrown
        with moss and mountain cranberries as to resemble
a mass of coarse basketwork. Once, his foot slumps, and he looks
        ten feet down into a bear's den, where the bears are
even now holed up at home. He seems to tread a garden of evil,
        the most porous and treacherous terrain, perhaps pontoon,
he has ever traveled. Still, not a twig snaps under his weight.
        Silent flocks of boulders meet him with hard, gray eyes.

Far below, the wide Maine country ruffles and flows like a woman's skirts.

    3.

When he returns, he finds his companions booked at a sad hotel—
        a damp shelf of rock beside a savage torrent.
One man is sick, rolled in a wool blanket of oblivion. The rest cling
        to a spitting fire, while frigid wind-spirits rush and roar
through the ravine all night. The men feel as naked and puny as
        newborn mice enthralled by a whirlwind, their lives in question
before dim vision clears. At midnight, the embers of the dreary fire
        suddenly explode and disperse. A bedfellow, startled
from drowse by a blazing fir-tree, imagines the world is on fire.

In the morning, after a plug of raw pork, a wafer of stale bread,
        and a dipper of condensed cloud, the shaken party
begins to inch up the falls, this time veering towards the tallest peak.
        Once again his companions lag far behind the flatlander,
seeming to quiver away from the mountain. For more than a mile,
        he climbs over huge and loosely-poised rocks that pause
within the clouds. Inscrutable, the summit lurks in silence behind a mist.
        From time to time, a rain of rocks hurls down the mountainside,
coming nowhere to rest, but changed to rockingstones set in motion.

After harsh hours, the solitary climber enters the skirts of a cloud
        that drifts across the summit but never disappears.
As fast as it flows away, it regenerates in the high cold air.
        It occurs to him that he's been swallowed by a hostile force
in which all nature is altered while the wind rises and falls.
        The most the cloud reveals is gray, dawning light,
an occasional flash of a dark, damp crag, then blindness once more.
        Could this be the Caucasus where, like the bound
Prometheus, he will feed screams to a night-bird slivering his chest?

Usually straight as an arrow, his reason flounders into the shadows.
        Vast Nature has caught him alone and unawares, and like
a common thief, it steals away his human allotment of divinest sense.

Unlike the spirit of the plains, this unsmiling Nature demands:
Why came ye here before your time? Is it not enough that I smile in the valleys?
I have never made this soil for thy feet, this air for thy breathing....
Too late, he realizes his insult in trespassing into this high place—
        the error of an insolent, civilized man, not of the native.
The furious mountain strikes the foot of any who'd step on its summit.

For the first time in his life, Thoreau feels an intense fear of Nature.
        So close to the mountain's summit, he retreats in shame
and descends without triumph. Grasping for a reason, he tells himself
        his companions will want to reach the river before nightfall;
therefore he must not cause delay. As he edges down, the wind
        brushes his cheek more benignly; the forests open their vistas.
Through trees, scattered lakes gleam like a shattered mirror caught by sun.
        Sharp fragments of granite blown by the wind, sparrows flit
to and from his face. The others laze below. Ktaadn's head clears.

Bee in a Jar

Two years in woods,
an elegy and a pastoral.
Wrought books
to pry the lid off

the pent ambitions of
anyone but him.
Should he concede more
to his own rule

of success?
Though it's always been
glassy vision not light fame
that teases him like

a bee in a jar.
He'd gone to the woods
to discover "life."
Now the woods

shy him back
on torn beating wings
for the sake
of Emerson's wife.

Man of the House

When Emerson sails from Boston to London
on the *Washington Irving,* his Concord friends gather
at the wharf on the fifth of October 1847
to seal their last sight of him on land's edge.
Touring the tiny stateroom with a keyhole window,
they lap up an eager dollop of his adventure.
When the division of passengers and stay-at-homes comes,
Abba Alcott's red face floods with hot tears.
Bawling like a lost heifer on the dock,
she startles strangers who take her for Emerson's wife.
But Lidian stands tearless with Thoreau behind the crowd.
As the packet slides away then slowly diminishes
to a point on the horizon,
the watchers on the wharf turn with vague relief
toward their own familiar land.

In silence Henry and Lidian ride back
to the big white Concord house on Lexington Road.
During this widowed year, he has promised
to live with her and be her general protector.
Another life to live. No more Walden.
With dolphin arches and flows, the buggy jounces
over sandy roads full of dry vernal ruts.
Thoreau prickles with awareness of her
meditative silence, how she bathes almost mystically in it.
At home (for he may now call it his home),
he gets to work outside, banking the trees against winter.
After repairing the white picket fence,
he sweats at the heavy task of cutting and splitting
the twenty-four cords of wood Mr. Emerson has ordered.
As winter sets in, his industry moves inside.
He installs closet shelves where Lidian wants them.
He sorts out Emerson's tangled railroad shares.
He straightens out the wrangle over land ownership
at the Fruitlands commune, for which Emerson is a trustee.

When spring comes, he manures and plants Emerson's fields,
including watermelon at Emerson's request.

In all this time, he teaches and mentors the children
Ellen, Edith, and Edward—eight, six, and three—
while their dead brother Waldo informs them
like a bright star glimmering through clouds.
Going about his householder's business,
he often carries Eddy fastened onto his shoulders.
For the little girls, he makes pan-pipes of pumpkin stalks and willow shoots.
At day's end, he gathers them around a fire for his stories
of a turtle-duel in the river, of a battle between ant-armies,
of his own childhood.
He thrills them with his sleight-of-hand magic tricks.
Finding a copper bed-warmer in the attic,
he fills it with red Indian corn and shakes it over a fire
until its metal heart pounds.
When the lid is lifted, white popcorn-blossoms burst
into the children's greedy hands.
Every season finds him filled with special plans,
none more exciting than foraging the land for wild fruits—
blueberries, barberries, chestnuts, purple grapes—
most of which vanish before the explorers reach home.
Once, with a steady grip, he picks up a sunning snake.
Guiding small hands over its dry scales,
he explains why the snake is better alive than killed.
On warm days he settles the children into his boat on the pond.
Striking an oar to the wooden side, he summons echoes for them.
Wrapping small arms around his sweat-sweet neck
one day, little Eddy whispers:
"Mr. Thoreau, will you be my father?"
Silence and a closer embrace. With a pang,
he writes to Emerson in London, warning that
he must come home to his children.

Quiet Lidian feels and regrets Thoreau's love—
though not his share in a remade family.

Eventually her husband writes to his "Queenie,"
"Our Spartan-Buddhist Henry is a *Pere* or *bon-homme malgre lui*, and it is a great comfort daily to think of him there with you."

Morning Star

> *The sun is but a morning star.*
> *—Henry David Thoreau*

Chaste twilights become the grey mourning dove,
Hovering near her children, not quite left
Alone. Dark Lidian, the loner's love,
Whitens with the morning cloudbank that sifts
And dissolves in a garish sun. Now he
Makes pan-pipes from willow stalks for her girls
And swings her boys, shoulder high, to the sky.
Tells them stories of valorous battles
Between ant soldiers, makes pencils and knives
Vanish by magic, then tickles behind
Small ears. Little Eddy almost believes
Him his father, his long arms feel so kind.
    Pere malgre lui, sneers her husband in London
    As a star guards her skies, dusk into dawn.

The Lovesong of Miss Sophia Foord

I really had anticipated no such foe as this in my career.
                                                  –Henry David Thoreau

Pudgy-plump Sophia Foord wrinkles her sallow nose
while engraving her love letter.
Perhaps facial cramps will hone her blunt pen into an arrow fit
to penetrate the heart of her beloved.
O, her dearly beloved!
Her pen scrawls across the page, ox-bowing a river
of love for her chosen mate—her lover (if only he would be),
her doted-upon, the darling soulmate
of her generous bosom, her intended whose liquid eyes surely
have kissed her phantom in undress time out of mind.
Her thick fingers tighten over the pen.
At her climactic proposal, she mutters in French, *Courage!*
Then, afterthoughts and misgivings.
So many reversals in her forty-five years,
she sometimes questions
whether birth began her wrong. But
how finely their lives might flow as one through remaining years.
Separate streams of loneliness, enjoining,
braiding each to each and the whole of Nature.
Procreating passion, if not children.
The sighs of Miss Foord heave so heavily that
the damp fragrant letter flies
from her shelf of calico and rumples at her foot.

Pressing the precious paper on the desk,
she rocks back in her chair and savors
soft thoughts of how Fate had tied him to her, slowly.
First, when she was elected tutor for the Alcott clan.
Again, when the Emerson and Channing children
entered her schoolmarm's fold.
Then, stupendous, when they carved her schoolroom and bedroom
from one end of Emerson's barn.

Of all the handymen in Concord,
the great man hired *him* to build a chimney to keep her warm!
Halcyon days, when that brick-and-mortar tower rose
through his hands, his bodily exertion, his designing mind!
Recalling his shyness at passing her quilted bedstead,
how his sky-gray eyes shifted everywhere in vain,
Miss Foord shudders with pleasure.
How sweetly he avoided her personal things,
like smoke rising from a smoldering fire.
O my dear, she gasps, our marriage was
ordained from that moment!
Miss Foord's brown eyes turn mud with passion.
She remembers the children as go-betweens.
Thinks of the crucial day she'd led them across Flint's pond
with boots and bloomers held like white flags in the air,
splashing among the fishes to the other side.
Still wet through, they came through the woods
"bawling and singing like crazy folks,"
according to sharp little Louisa.
Love of Nature has wed more souls than not.
Yes, he must reply. *Yes!*

      *** *** ***

Shocked and appalled, Thoreau drops the letter like poison.
Then in November 1847, he finally informs Emerson in England
of Miss Foord's proposal:
I did not write a deliberate answer.
How could I deliberate upon it? I sent back
as distinct a <u>no</u> as I have learned to pronounce. . . .

The immortal voice of Ralph Waldo Emerson
trumpets a royal "we" across the Atlantic,
promising to snuff her lugubrious lovesong forever:
You tell me in your letter one odious circumstance,
which we will dismiss from remembrance henceforward–

But the yearning song will not be stilled!
In February 1849, Aunt Maria Thoreau writes Prudence Ward:
By the way, have you heard
what a strange story there was about Miss Ford, and Henry,
Mrs. Brooks said at the convention,
a lady came to her and inquired, if it was true,
that Miss F– had committed, or was going to commit
suicide on account of H– Thoreau, what a ridiculous story this is.

In November, warm with glee,
Aunt Maria scribbles out further news:
Miss Foord has gone crazy!
She sends Henry incoherent letters citing—
British steamers—dreadful shipwrecks on the ocean—
which he puts right into the fire.

   *** *** ***

Pudgy-plump Sophia Foord soldiers on, a spinster
weathering suicide, insanity, obsession,
and a maddening inability to expel the lovesong
from her buzzing brain.
She may justly blame Fate for her virtue.
On the rebound,
she gets herself hired as a governess
by Elizabeth Buffam Chace, an abolitionist
(Henry's cause)
from Valley Falls, Rhode Island.
The little Chaces never forget
the dark-skinned, pudgy-faced woman
who confided to their mother that
Thoreau's soul was a twin to her own,
and that their two spirits would finally be
united on the other side.
Twenty years beyond her designated lover's death,
antiquated, scandalous Sophia Foord still
provides fodder for gossips.

Her constant contralto still sallies forth
above the gossip-chorus,
even above his sister Sophia's whinny to Ellen Sewall Osgood,
the first love of Henry Thoreau.
Thankfully, at last Miss Foord's queer old ears hear,
not her ancient lovesong, but a welcoming lyre.
All her long wars over,
transfigured,
she sees the union saved.

The Lecture Wars

"I wish Henry could find something better to do
than walking off every now and then,"
snuffles Aunt Maria Thoreau.
Papering, whitewashing, budding, hoeing,
wood-sawing, pencil-making—all mean cash.
But for doing something, they lack class.
He prints handbills to drum up more land-survey.
Pay is better, and work gets him away.

But it strikes him that a quicker income
and fame—a la Emerson—is in the lyceum.
Why shouldn't he also live by hawking
his intellectual harvest on the road?
In the fall of 1848, with Emerson's help,
he starts to lecture with astonishing success.
In Salem, his notes on economy thrill Sophia
Hawthorne so that her ears ring. To her

Mr. Thoreau seems "as gentle, simple,
ruddy, and meek as all geniuses should be."
His "great blue eyes," she confesses,
"put into shade" his "uncomely" Gallic nose.
Listening to him, Mrs. H. feels herself airily
"wandering through copse and dingle."
Alas, Sophia is not the critic to rival
more jaded writers of lecture reviews.

The *Salem Observer* finds him Emersonian enough
for a native product, exuding "some" charm.
But in Greeley's *Tribune,* a "Mr. Thorough" slams
his "crablike cold and snailish existence."
To the *Worcester Palladium*, he shows how silly
the human mind can be. His philosophy makes
no one the wiser—a wheelbarrow rolled by
an Irishman renders a better service.

Aunt Maria Thoreau is mortified.
Her nephew, a clown harping on a hill of beans!
She washes her hands. Claims she's
as disgusted by his antics as the papers are.
Like Worcester, she's had enough of feckless,
arrogant, bean-counting Henry Thoreau.
But, thanks to H. G. O. Blake, an odd stick,
they invite him back to make more people sick.

On the Concord and the Merrimack

An elegy for his brother,
ten years in making.
A flurry
of bland misreadings.

A river voyage,
a slender thread with
too big beads & ingots
strung on it.

A New England fragrance
of woods and streams,
unwritable
anywhere else.

Blasphemy.
Pantheistic egotism.
It does not delight either
Aunt Maria or Horace Greeley.

A hammock book,
fit only
for the idleness
of summer malaise.

Sneers at his
seven hundred copies,
stored in the attic.
Fool wrote a book. Sold

not one. Now
he combs his hair with
a pine cone
and haunts his house.

Thy Indelible Mild Eye Is My Sky

On the death of Helen Thoreau, June 14, 1849

In her eyes, a sky of changing waters,
he sees his sister fade as if she's slipped
to another room to find her treasures
of clotted paints, played-upon keys, frayed books.
He waits. It's all too clear, what's done is done.
Her life, her brilliance, sacrificed for schools
that used her up on needlepoint lessons
for dull rich girls. An ancient shame, normal
neglect of her promise, her wasting worth.
Now, this wasted flesh. Rotting, consumptive
rise and fall, tearing from earth to earth
like a hard birth, rending cold death alive.
    At parlor rites, he's mute while preachers vie,
    then stands to let her music box unwind.

The Yellow House on Main Street

The death of a daughter
requires a new house.
Raised ceilings, brightening
sidelit doors, porticoes.

In her new yellow house
on Main Street,
paid-for by plumbago,
Mrs. Cynthia knows.

As if the royal queen
were due for tea,
she hires two Irish girls
to serve and clean.

Her moody son,
now called *Thoreau* as if
the only one,
keeps well to himself.

His attic shelves
hold books, nests, eggs,
gray-lace lichens,
mauls and arrowheads,

rocks, pebbles, rippled
volumes of dried plants.
Sloping walls save Abenaki
snowshoes and deer-antlers.

His Walden cot, one bureau,
two chairs are all, but for a perennial
dust, thick as Irish moss,
no maid will touch.

V.

My life, my life! why will you linger?
Are the years short and the months of no account?

–Henry David Thoreau

Whitman's Room

Two gray ghosts lying in Whitman's mussed sheets
invite the full return of their bodies.
Hercules, Bacchus, and a Satyr
leer and flex their expansive biceps and bulges
from a picture pinned on the soot-stained wallpaper.
Strewn lavishly across the mantlepiece,
Whitman's well-used books with broken spines
ache to end it all in the ashes.
A lidless yellow eye glares
out of a porcelain chamberpot
left unceremoniously in the middle of the room.

Thoreau glares into the pee-pot with disgust,
but its chipped white shoulders will
neither flinch nor shrug.
Was it Emerson's or Alcott's idea to drag him down
to Brooklyn to meet this Walt Whitman?
And why is a Quaker lady from Philadelphia here?
Pushing about a corset of voluminous breasts
and gazing over them benevolently
into the chamberpot?
The room of the infamous loafer-poet!
The room stinks, really stinks.
How unlike his own mother's house,
Thoreau thinks, noting ruefully that he, too,
lives with his mother, off and on.

Transcendentalists awkwardly bumble about,
elbowing unwashed plates and cups.
Attempting to say something arcane,
they back into dust-choked litters of manuscripts.
Thoreau finds an angular oak chair.
Walt reclines into his own flowery rat's-nest,
pops open a button over his belly, ignores it,
and then talks. And talks. Of his own greatness.

Of his greatness, synonymous with the cosmos, apparently.
The greatness of his unbelievable baths in midwinter.
The greatness of his habitual rides atop an omnibus,
up and down Broadway from morning to night.
The greatness of his dining with whipsters, after.
The greatness of his three muses on the wall, signifying One Great Walt.
The greatness of his luscious nights at the opera in New York.
The greatness of his fine editing of the *New Orleans Crescent*.
The greatness of his leisurely mornings, spent reading and writing.
The greatness of his afternoons, spent inspecting every crevice of beloved Brooklyn.
Amazingly, he appears incurious except to wonder
what do the Brahmins say about his great book, *Leaves of Grass*.
Before anyone constructs a reply,
he blows on about Emerson's letter in confidence to him,
greeting him at the start of a Great Career.
Of course he's published those words everywhere!

Under the cold cold moon, Thoreau's *Walden*
ponders a chosen solitude.

Face to face, suspicious and opposed,
Nature's two declared lovers
lock liquid gray eyes beneath drooping, sensual lids.
Alarmed, Emerson and Alcott struggle
but fail to bridge an ocean of mistrust between the two writers.
Thoreau eyes the poet's rumpled and smelly blue shirt,
a costume for the common man.
But those soft hands never did a day's work, he believes.
Breaking through a brief silence in Whitman's gab,
he blurts that if the sensual mass of men
can possibly feel ashamed of themselves,
they have good reason to be so.
Look at this—*this Brooklyn*. Its political corruption.
Is *this* the stuff of celebration?
He waves a callous, dismissive hand.

Wounded, Whitman defends the city of his poetry.

He insists that Thoreau misapprehends.
Thoreau insists otherwise.
To each other, they will not be Henry and Walt.
As verbal war threaten to break out,
the Quaker lady from Philadelphia rises majestically
and squashes pugilism with her peace:
a weighty dissertation on great lions of literature.
As the gray November day fades into a grim chill,
the ambassadors depart from Whitman's room.
Trundling down the unlit shoddy stair,
Thoreau is heard to mutter,
That is a Great Man.

Later Whitman will brag about meeting
the great Thoreau—it was somewhere in Concord, as he recalls.

The Irish Graveyard at Grampus Rock

At the port of Boston, travelers watch the sea
with vague mistrust, frowning
at chained timepieces drawn from vests.
Overdue, the Provincetown packet appears
nowhere on the thrashing waves.
Perhaps, in the aftermath of October's hurricane,
the captain prefers the Cape's clutch
to the sinews and claws of combative tides.
An alarm erupts in the crowd.
Like a crier, a man is shouting news from a handbill
being passed into snatching hands.
> *Death! One hundred forty-five lives lost at Cohasset.*

Sailing in from Galway, the brig *St. John* has cracked
an iron-clad eggshell over Grampus Rock.
A yolk of Irish emigrants has slipped into a whirl of waves.
Now the would-be packeteers rush back to merge
with Boston-Irish hordes already in the cars to Cohasset.
As fish to a lure, all rush towards disaster
to see if any human effigies remain on the beach.
From the moving train, a passel of fishermen are seen
shoveling a muddy cellar-hole in the Cohasset graveyard.
At the station, Thoreau and his companion are swept along
with hundreds of people swelling over the Common
with guns, game-bags, and baying hounds.

On the beach road to Pleasant Cove,
the crowd clashes with a fleet of farm wagons and hay-rigs
loaded with coffins packed like salt cod.
On the littered beach, men are nailing down lids
while, just ahead of them, people lift loose white sheets
to peer at the tangle inside each deal box.
No sign of grief is visible.
Businesslike,
every hand is engaged in sorting and transit.

Those who would keen for the rags, feathers, and straw bonnets
live across the sea and do not know.

Thoreau moves on down the beach,
aware of how smooth the sea has washed the sand.
Wiped its slate clean.
Among the marble feet and matted hair,
he encounters a drowned girl, an image of a once-girl
that fastens in his mind for life.
Gashed muscles and bones laid open,
now she is a butchered hulk of red and white,
the prey of rocks, worms, fishes.
Unseeing eyes stare at the New World they'd looked for,
without terror, timidity, or regret.
No doubt she was meant to go out to service.
To scrub and dust some American house.
He remembers the bleeding knuckles of the Irish girls
as they heaved dripping wet blankets over his mother's line.
Half-concealed by swollen flesh,
he glimpses a thin string clinging to the freckled neck.
Some emblem or talisman.
Let it remain. Let it remain. Let it remain.

The corpse of the *St. John* itself
sprawls in a flowery spray of petals across Cohasset.
Iron braces lie, snapped like driftwood.
Forty-foot timbers, thrown high over the dunes,
are so rotten that Thoreau thrusts his umbrella through.
Afloat, the *St. John* was a ship of death.
Thoreau slogs on towards Whitehead,
where an old man and his son with a team of Belgian horses
are loading rockweed, kelp, and seaweed into a wagon.
For pumping life back into salt sand, nothing beats green manure.
But it must be claimed at once,
before the sea snatches back its green gift.

Fire Island

    1. The Wreck of the *Elizabeth*

Laden with marble carved from a hill in Carrara,
the *Elizabeth* sways against mountainous waves,
running before a hurricane in the north Atlantic.
Blind night masks precipices of sea
leaping high around the masts and whirling
down to the ocean floor. Panther-wind screams through
the pounding and parting quake of the sea.
And the crew of the *Elizabeth* cower and shrink.
Is that the light for Navesink?
Fierce with terror and desire, the untried
captain-standing-in seizes on any hope of safe harbor.
If only he'd stayed in Italy, not stood in for the dead man
who should have commanded this ship.
Surely, now, they've entered the map's blank space
between Barnegat and Cape May. Surely, if prayers hold power
over the hellish pitch and boiling sea, that glimmer of light
is—must be—Navesink.

No waiting for daylight to make sure. So anxious is he
that he orders the prow aimed straight for the long, low bars
underlying the sea the length of Fire Island.
At 3:30 A. M., hell's hour, the brig veers and strikes,
pitching passengers out of their bunks and stunning the crew.
The next wave picks up the stern, swings it around like a child's toy,
and slams the massive ship broadside onto the bar.
One dreadful shudder, then a roar.
The Carrara marble, all one hundred and fifty tons of it,
has broken loose from the hold.
Every last ton, meant for obelisques and busts, not graves,
rams clean through the ship's side.
Whited marble, a sepulcher of nursery blocks tumbled below
the bellow of the hurricane, the hollow ship teeters
on the ledge of a black green maw,
a globe of fractured glass.

2. Smith Oakes, Thief

His wife's shrill caws wake Smith Oakes, thief,
at dawn on July 19, 1850. Little he knows, or cares. Then—
Ship aground! He jumps clear out of bed. Those
lovely words thrill every bone in him. Besotted
bones of sailors, mothers, fathers, babies—all
leave their luck to him, as finally as any will and testament.
Hobbling into his trousers as he runs,
he makes out the *Elizabeth*, lurching like a cow in quicksand
barely two-hundred yards offshore.
A familiar company of rogues have beat him to it,
milling around with torches and carts.
But the breaking-up has still to come, and Smith Oakes
licks his lips and gauges the power of the breakers
against the flooding ship.
Scuttling sideways on the sand, killing time,
he knows how events are unfolding aboard the fragment.
How the usual hysteria wends toward the rapture.
Even now, some drenched white rag of a bedsheet or nightgown
tethered to the mainmast can be seen, blowing to shreds.
Look to the tide, Oakesy love, his wife cries:
brassbound trunks, desks, crates of almonds, an Italian melon, a bustled petticoat,
swirling, roll in—

3. The Ossolis

Since childhood, Margaret has dreamed
of her death by water.
Horrible, ghoulish nightmares
that fluttered her myopic squinty eyes
in the telling. Counting the ways she'd dreamed
of drowning bore her down,
defied her rational education, made her feel
the onus of femaleness.
Margaret the prodigy, her father's favorite before
her fall from grace as a lumpish teen.

Disgusting, slope-shouldered, fat, female,
she lost herself in writing.
Later, expected to support
her mother, brothers, sister, she fled
to Italy, a thin middle-aged spinster, hoping
to produce a saleable tome on the Roman Revolution.
And she did, while also succumbing
to the youth and beauty of Ossoli
and reproducing her shame and wonder
with the birth of Nino.

Still, in spite of good sex and bad colic,
the plague of death by water
continues to haunt her almost nightly.
Even in the common light of day,
stark-naked terror has begun to seize her,
now that she contemplates sailing back to America,
no longer a bluestocking old maid,
but with her adorable double-burden of
an illegitimate child and an unemployable marchese.

    4. The Emissary

Because Emerson is too distraught to go,
five days after the horrific wreck of the *Elizabeth*
within mere yards of Fire Island,
Henry Thoreau enters the shanty of Smith Oakes.
Humanely, someone must inquire
for the remains of Margaret Fuller and her child,
and even for that Italian.
And he must find out if there's any hope
of retrieving her greater child to come—
the manuscript of her big book.
She has conspired in the Roman Revolution,
has been its amanuensis or scribe—surely
some waterlogged shred of her great mind's produce survives?

All simpering smiles and sympathy,
Smith Oakes and his cockle-faced wife present
a grand display of Margaret's brassbound trunks, "tragically"
emptied of her gold watch and pages "by the sea."
Unaware of his guest's anger, the scavenger gabbles on,
pausing only to spit tobacco at the fire.
With the wreck of the *St. John* and the drowned Irish girl,
only eight months before, and now this shock to absorb,
Thoreau turns his back without a word.
Walking down the beach, he is shaken by nature's calm
after such a gross natural disaster.
Now Margaret will live in history, not for her worth,
but as a drama-queen in a drenched nightdress,
a half-clad mother clinging to her babe—and losing—
against a wild sea. A subject for
half-baked etchings hung in moldy parlors.
He moves down the caked sand, remembering her
on that summer day on Walden Pond.
Damselfly-fingers drizzling water-tension as he rested the oars.
She'd told him then of her nightmares,
of the obscene ways she'd met death by water.
Five miles down the beach, he stoops beside a torn blue coat.
An Italian nobleman's coat. Ossoli's coat. He rips off a button.
That remains—and a skeleton with only a pound of flesh left to lose.
The dead possess the shore as the living cannot.

Margaret's Ghost

Ripped from the sand-clogged coat of Ossoli
on the smashed Fire Island shore, a button
Thoreau studies between finger and thumb
eclipses the sun. To think, this brass key
outlasts all lost lives connected with it:
Ossoli's heart, Margaret's breath, Nino's
baby handclap and drool. He can't suppose
matter means much at all, comparing grit
with dream. In life he'd never warmed to her.
But her blue silk dreams had stormed a man's world.
Fought patterns meant to cut her down to size.
Thought and passion ruled the woman, so far
as he knew. She was human. Scandal sold.
    Ossoli's button escapes truth *and* lies.

On First Looking at Lake Champlain, Thoreau Sees Water

At Vergennes,
the conquered lake lies
calm as a pond.

French-laced
waves
retrace its name in

blue-black wash,
flooding from
some leaky pen.

Champlain ruled here
for France.
But making the lake

an eternal postcard
of himself—
was this too dire

a pride?
White gulls, feathered
schooners, mull

between blue green
ridges, floating
from shore to shore

one pale September
evening when
Thoreau meditates

the long water from
a rattling train.
His dim view of the lake

challenges twilight
to redact all airs
assumed by *le seigneur*.

At the Cathedral of Notre Dame in Montreal

An echo rebukes every step he takes to the altar.
Two women, brooding alone, do not raise their eyes
nor do they regard each other as he passes.
A crowd of muddy Frenchmen in gray homespun,
who'd got off the steamboat behind him,

clump in. With a deal of boot-scuffling, like cattle
trying to lie down, they buckle to their knees in the aisle
before the crucified Christ. Drawing back, Thoreau
pictures a herd of oxen strayed into an empty cathedral,
struggling to orient filthy hides and hooves.

Goat-agile himself, he looks a long way down his nose.
Their physical reverence repels his idea of peace.
He, too, could kneel. Some fine Monday.
For now, he'll keep off. If he had a prayer, it rose
over an angry, enchafed sea. Angle and wheel of wings.

Wild Apples

From haggard trees, dying since
his boyhood but not yet dead,
he expects a late flourish.
Now is the time for wild apples.

Among hissing high weeds
and winds teasing bud-tips down,
the lichen-clad trunks gnarl and twist.
Yet, fierce wine-sap surges

until the wild old trees
strew the ground with red and gold.
Deserted by farmers, drilled
by woodpeckers, the abandoned

orchard waves to him.
Faith bids him to look again
beneath their boughs. Blush, beauty,
apple of the evening skies.

Wild Man

What hope is there for any human
afraid of the woods?
Thoreau rants to his journal,
warehouse for field-gnarled notes.
He has eaten the wild apples.

He rails. What hope *is* there
for anyone who is afraid of the woods,
the solitude, the darkness?
Has he been too much with Hawthorne—
whose dank forest oozes?

Is not God silent and mysterious?
Shy of church socials? Ladies fear silence
worse than sin. Nowhere in the voluble machine,
God is everywhere in the wild.
An echoing axe in the mind's woods.

Hewing his canoe for the rapids.

In His Thirty-Fourth Year, Thoreau Hears the Music of Time

He tramps the deserted fields and woods
of Concord. Wayland. Acton.
Bedford, Boxboro, Billerica.
Lincoln, Natick, Sudbury, Stow.
Circling villages, crossing narrow musky roads
tamped by foxes and minks.

His Vermont gray and browns and greens
blend with pastures stippled
with withering sweet-fern and lechea.
Under his arm, he grips *Primo Flauto*, his father's
rippled music book, for pressing flowers.
In his other hand, a gnarled cane shaved flat

for marking off in inches and feet.
His hat with a built-in shelf, size 7, preserves
delicate botanical specimens—his brains, he jests,
require keeping fresh and moist.
Heedless of critics, he explores the unpathed ways
while a raw question turns in his mind.

He has come to believe no synchronicity exists
between himself and nature. That his own seasons
revolve unnaturally slower than nature's wheel.
Less measureably than the calendar pinned
to his mother's kitchen wall. Budded in prelude,
his spirit wilts. Will its unfolding slow, then cease,

unlike nature's quickness? His moods exert a power
to persuade or dissuade him. Hovering low,
they cloud and shadow thought. By sheer will,
he steps to a steadfast inward rhythm. Though
he wanders the countryside like a homeless tramp,
picking and eating all varieties of wild apples.

In a literal way, he detaches himself from nature.
Places it under a microscope to take a colder measure.
Compiles lists, catalogs, Latin names of plants, e. g.,
the spotted spurge (*Euphorbia maculata*), out of blossom.
In September, he meanders slowly perforce
through thicketed fields, waist-high in goldenrod,

striving after some lighter tone. Semblance of sanity.
Aching to see simply and cleanly once more.
Shipwreck and the sight of human flotsam haunt his mind.
He feels as if he had committed suicide.
Wings blackened and bent, his Pegasus
has turned into a reptile groveling on its belly.

Through long nights into day, he lolls in the river
among the shallows while weed-slime waves
across his inert body. He bathes. In a few hours,
he bathes again, then again. Never wet enough.
A bundle of clothes slung over his back,
he treads the river endwise. In the nude. To no end.

Walking to Three Friends' Hill one late afternoon,
he feels the strengthening winds of autumn blow
through an Aeolian telegraph-harp, and himself.
In the Deep Cut, he pauses as the music increases,
where its tones splay to variations with the tension held
in different parts of the wire. As he listens closely,

every pore of the green-gold woods moistens and brightens,
and rustles more strongly with strains of music.
Every swell and inflection threads the woods,
pouring through every green cell, as from
a divine tree, a divine mass of trees. Saturate, he feels
a wild measure saving his mind from rot.

Snake Summer

His noiseless passage through Britton's clearing
on a coolly dazzling autumn afternoon
surprises a thick, loosely-looped blacksnake
basking on a rocky flare of sun-bake.
With no change of expression in its hard
yellow dragon's eyes, the snake raises
its long head with threatening calm just before
the dry brush explodes into vicious thrashing.
An astounding length of lustrous horsewhip
vanishes into a shuddering green-black briar.

Through dull waning days, he surveys lots
for men who fell the solemn trees and build.
His flawless work, a depressing paid complicity.
Coming home one winter evening, he sees
a sunset without the sun. Just a pale white
fire, descending over the trembling black pines.
For a frozen moment, it is snake summer.
He could thank this shortened shrift of time.
Whole skies will be shut out by snow clouds.
Snow on snow will console his blue gray eye.

Chess-Boxers

> *–My dear Henry,*
> *A frog was made to live in a swamp,*
> *but a man was not made to live in a swamp.*
> *Yours ever,*
> *R.*

Sweeping a hand,
Emerson laments the dirth
of great living poets.
Meditating his own words,
he awaits the homage of
sycophants in his parlor.

Thoreau retorts:
He's found a great poet
singing in the woods.
But he wears a feather coat
and hasn't been to Harvard.
Sycophants clear their throats.

Emerson: *Let us cage it.*
Thoreau: *That is just the way*
the world spoils its poets.
Emerson leaves to dine.
Thoreau walks back to the woods.
Sycophants scribble a score.

Thoreau Leaves the Party

When Hayward's Pond is iced all over
unexpectedly, he's roped into going
to a house-party. A bad place to go.

Thirty or forty persons, mostly young
women, squall about in a parlor-cage
of tropical heat and noise. Skulking,

he smacks into the breasts of a girl
who flies at him with the loquacity of
a spring chickadee. Drily polite,

he fends off her nestward flutterings.
Instantly he's pierced by another fine eye.
Since he rarely looks folks in the face,

he wouldn't know. The shrill shackles him
so tightly now though that he can't avoid
the alarming motion of tinted female lips,

closing in. Featherbed-heat swells up.
A mating-dance whirs and claps at his ear.
Pert women alight and take flight so that

he can't be sure if they are real, or not.
Yet, when he slips home alone across the ice,
desire flies to one shy bird, settled for life.

The Quiet Man

The small quiet man who was his father
slipped away without much of an ado.
After rehearsing fond farewells to them
two or three times, no doubt he'd felt sheepish
or impatient with his wife's lavish grief.
His deaf ear, turned so often in recourse
to an endless stream of female chatter,
had turned deaf in fact, and now, unhearing.
Surprised by tears, Thoreau oddly recalls
the dead horse abandoned in Walden Woods.
How he'd had to take the long way around
to endure its dust-bound processional.
    And yet, he'd felt a lift of gladness for
    the poor animal returning to home.

The Moose Hunt

At fuming daybreak, bands of cold light
rifle without hope among the rag-tag pines.
Mutely, the hunters trek along the Penobscot.
Once in a while, they glimpse distant Katahdin
between dripping mists and storm-torn limbs.
Shortly after noon—when in September it seems
that the continental climate abruptly reverses—
they spot two moose on the edge of a meadow.
Peering through alders, Thoreau is struck by
their resemblance to rabbits. Twitching long ears,
half-frightened inquisitive eyes. *God's own horses*—

Swiftly his cousin from Bangor loads and fires.
The young one leaps into the stream, cowering
in confusion, uttering two or three squeaks.
The image plants itself in Thoreau's mind until
death. The old moose pauses for an instant
atop the bank to look back at her shivering calf,
then dashes into the woods. Before he knows it,
the second shot has blasted the air around him.
The calf hesitates, thrashes in the water, then
gangles up the bank, crashing through the maze
with wild directionless terror.

An hour after Joe Aitteon, the Indian guide,
had seized his hatchet and sped off, tracking
the clue of *a single drop of blood on the handsome,
shining leaves of the Clintonia borealis*—they stumble
on the velvet cow by pure chance, lying dead
but still warm, in the middle of the stream's
switchback toward the rapids. Her water-swollen
body palpitates when Joe knifes under the skin.
Warm milk flows in streams from her torn udder.
From her robe, a ghastly red carcass emerges.
Thoreau's Bangor cousin lopes after the calf.

Fugitive Justice

    1.

Before visiting his cousins
in Bangor, Maine,
he had never seen a moose.

Then he saw two at once,
peering shyly through the alders.
Then he saw them in frenzy,

pursued through tangled trees.
Then he saw a lurid gleam in the forest—
a naked red carcass

left for maggots and wolves.
Through his revulsion,
he believes

the enormous cow-spirit in velvet
will return through mist-clouds
to feed her starving calf.

    2.

The local Irish who fled
the potato famine of the 1840s
at first seem to him

dirty and bereft
of any spiritual intuitions,
the way his cousin saw the moose.

Then by chance
he encounters Johnny Riordan,
who is only five,

trudging a snowy mile to school
wearing patches, not coat,
and holes, not shoes.

He is flustered
until he takes a warm new cloak
to the little boy.

And, in reaching out
to the low Irish,
he discovers a literate family.

He takes to wearing sturdy
clay-colored trousers
of Irish corduroy himself,

to the disgust of respectable folk.
He stands up, too, for those
oppressed "Paddies,"

Michael Flannery, Barney Mullins,
John Field, whose Yankee employers
deny them an honest wage.

    3.

October 1, 1851.
He buys a ticket
to Burlington, Vermont
for fugitive Henry Williams,
in flight to Canada.
Later he raises six-hundred dollars
to purchase and return him
to Boston, a free man.

November 1, 1853.

While the Thoreaus lodge
a free black woman in their home,
he collects money to purchase
her husband from a Mr. Moore
of Norfolk, Virginia.
First, Moore baits his price
at six-hundred dollars.
When the woman raises that sum,
she is told that the price
has switched to eight hundred.

    4.

His heart has bled for the oppressed,
animal and human alike.
He has hidden fugitives, washed them, fed them,
clothed them, nursed their wounds.
In all of this, his wonder increases to no end.
How is the harming of *any* creature of nature defensible?
What else will God require of *him*?

The Brown Defense

After the fire-storm attack at Harper's Ferry, Virginia,
after the blood-letting of too many sons,
after John Brown molders in his prison-cell
before moldering in a murderer's grave,
a Massachusetts man called Thoreau defends his virtue
in the name of resistance to an enslaving State.

First, he called for withholding taxes.
Next, he called for disobeying the Fugitive Slave Law.
Now, he calls for a direct and open rebellion against the State.
That which, in cold blood, John Brown has already done.
For mayhem, Brown will hang when his time is due.
Still the Concord man's cry rings out, pleading for the felon's life.

Has he only been swept up in the drama on a Concord stage?
When feisty John Brown had whipped out a big Bowie knife
seized from a Border Ruffian? Shown off the chains
he said slavers had used to bind his son? Has Thoreau thought—
does one sacred principle justify *any* act?

Knowing less than a babe about how the crazy old man
led the forces of destruction in the Pottawatomie massacre in Kansas,
he endorses the fire-brand's Apocalypse without qualms.
His sister and her friends piece a bed-quilt for the Widow Brown.
In gratitude, she presents to Thoreau her husband's long knife.

Autumnal Tints

Wild apples, wild huckleberries,
native dwellers, the past in autumnal tints—
his thoughts revert to cycles following the sacred bow,
leaving polemics to flat-earth people.

Now, on his daily walk around town,
he finds endless time. For a gossip, for telling a yarn.
Now, with his old rival in love and letters, he spends afternoons
rowing a calm water embossed by slant sun.

Cold

In the graying November of 1860,
he decides to record the aging patterns
of specific trees in specific groves.

Engrossed in measurement, he spends
a bitter December afternoon counting
the rings on stumps on Fair Haven Hill

until the cold drives him home, shaking.
It's plain he's caught his death; but still,
rather than be coddled at home, he passes

his evening debating with Sam Staples
about John Brown's sensational raid.
On the eleventh, despite the opposition

of his friends, his family, and his physician,
he travels to Waterbury, Connecticut
to read his "Autumnal Tints" to a crowd.

The sickness is so heavy that its weight
nearly closes him down. His dead delivery
in monotone annoys the restless audience.

"Dull" and "common-place," a critic yawns.
For troubling to fulfill the engagement,
he returns to Concord defeated and gravely ill.

For the rest of the winter he keeps to home,
feeling pent-up like a wounded peregrine.
His alter-ego, his journal, falls mute and still.

Minnesota

A shambling invalid for a housebound year, at last
he musters strength to stroll the Boston road
near Punkatasset Hill, where the bluebirds nested in February.
On the day of Lincoln's inauguration, March 4, 1861,
he scoffs at Alcott for blithely trusting
those duplicitous Republican men.
For his part, he plans to ignore the whole mean crowd.
Sick and tired, he wants to get on with his life.

But in mid-March, bitter cold and snow pen him in
again. His own blood can't warm him.
West Indies? Southern Europe? *Any* warmer climate?
Too muggy, too expensive, he rasps.
When someone recalls the Bangor cousin who'd moved
out to Minnesota for its drier air, he pounces.
A prime excuse to see wholly new American flora and fauna—
he's never been west of the Alleghenies!

But before he and Horace Mann's young son reach Albany,
he's already spent. From there on, it's merely
Thoreau at Niagara, Thoreau in Chicago, Dunleith, St. Paul.
Thoreau on the Mississippi steamboat *Itasca*.
Prairies, Indian dogs, pigs, encampments of Dacotah wigwams.
Chief Little Crow, dancers, flutes, a roasted ox.
Hoping to lay eyes on the wild crabapple in its native place,
he finds only a transplanted tree in withered flower.

On Mackinaw Island, young Mann eagerly explores on his own
while Thoreau shivers for five days by the campfire.
Finally they board the *Sun* and sail down through Lake Huron to Ontario.
They scramble onto trains to Toronto, to Boston, and finally to
Concord. July 9, 1861. A clear intuition invites him
to wind up his affairs. As it is, he won't live long enough
to know how soon his young friend will die of tuberculosis.
Caught, some claim, from Thoreau in Minnesota.

Wild Grapes

Near the end
of September 1861,
Thoreau and his sister Sophia
walk out to Walden Pond.
It's one of those
bright blue and gold days
that promises to last forever.
Yet, for all of its brilliance,
everything is changing.
While Sophia sketches
the place where he once
devoured himself alive,
thinking and writing,
Thoreau gathers a few
wild grapes into his hand.
Slowly, ruminating,
he drops them one by one
into the still water.
As each Concord orb
breaks through,
rings within rings of light
flood across the plain
of Walden.
By evening a flush comes
to his cheek,
a brightness and beauty
to his eyes,
painful to behold.

Up Country

A time for playing
with his sister Sophia's kittens.
Tiny whiskers, tiny teeth.
Papery skin snagged by tiny claws
drawing a crescent moon
of three red beads.

A time for scraping
spring frost from a windowpane.
Failing to clear a view
of changes in the seasonal world
beyond the glass, a world
he no longer sees.

A time for seeing
the world within a fluttering eye.
The hunted velvet moose
pausing to look back
at her frightened calf, before taking
her wound up country.

Acknowledgments

No poem in this volume could have been written without the works of Thoreau himself. I am especially grateful for access to the Damien Searls and the Carl Bode editions of selected *Journals* and for Bode's *Collected Poems of Henry Thoreau*. Invaluable as well are Thoreau's *Cape Cod; The Maine Woods; October, or Autumnal Tints; A Week on the Concord and the Merrimack; Walden;* and *Wild Fruits*. If any of my poems possess some power, Thoreau is the source.

Walter Harding's *The Days of Henry Thoreau* provided the biographical framework as well as a wealth of language and information which necessarily enters the poems. Ralph Waldo Emerson's journals revealed delicious insights into the changing relationship between the men. Other works about Thoreau and his circle which I found useful include books by Lydia Maria Child, John Matteson, Robert D. Richardson, Jr., and Harmon Smith, as well as the edited recollections of family, friends, and associates of Thoreau by Sandra Harbert Petrulionis.

I offer grateful thanks to the editors of the following publications in which some of my poems previously appeared: *Aurorian*, "Wild Apples" and "Wild Man," Fall 2015; *Blueline*, "From a Granite Ledge on Greylock, Thoreau Considers the Railroad," 2015; *The Fourth River*, "Dame School," Spring 2017; and *Northern Woodlands*, "Concord Spring 1845," Spring 2015.

Two of the poems were part of "The Language of Art," an exhibition by Edgewater Gallery, Middlebury, Vermont in April 2019. "The Husbandry Poet" and "Solitude" were paired with Margaret Gerding's oil paintings "Concord Farm" and "Cloud Layers II."

I am grateful to the Spring Street Poets of Middlebury, Vermont for their good advice and encouragement over the years.

To Marc Estrin and Donna Bister of the Fomite Press, I offer sincere appreciation and admiration for their abundant insight and skill in bringing this book to publication.

I reserve a special appreciation for Richard Potter, who first acquainted me with Thoreau's lines: "My life has been the poem I would have writ, / But I could not both live and utter it."

About the Author

Along with *Thoreau's Umbrella*, Janice Miller Potter has published the poetry collections *Meanwell* (Fomite, 2012) and *Psalms in Time* (Finishing Line, 2008). Her poems appear widely in journals, including P*oet Lore, Chiron Review, Connecticut Review, Worcester Review, Adirondack Review, Bloodroot, Northern Woodlands, Sow's Ear, Snowy Egret, Words & Images, roger, Café Review, The Salon, Aurorean, Blueline, The Fourth River, Blue Collar Review, Ruah, Christian Science Monitor, Larcom Review, Dusty Dog,* and *The Pittsburgh Quarterly* which awarded her its Sara Henderson Hay Prize in 2005. Her poems have been anthologized in *Birchsong: Poetry Centered in Vermont; Gathered: Contemporary Quaker Poets; Overtime: Punchin' Out with the Mill Hunk Herald* and elsewhere. Her Arthurian long-poem, "The Swans of Camelot," is part of The Camelot Project of the University of Rochester. Formerly an instructor of literature and writing at Rhode Island College, she lives in Cornwall, Vermont.

Fomite

About Fomite

A fomite is a medium capable of transmitting infectious organisms from one individual to another.

"The activity of art is based on the capacity of people to be infected by the feelings of others." Tolstoy, *What Is Art?*

Writing a review on Amazon, Good Reads, Shelfari, Library Thing or other social media sites for readers will help the progress of independent publishing. To submit a review, go to the book page on any of the sites and follow the links for reviews. Books from independent presses rely on reader to reader communications.

For more information or to order any of our books, visit
http://www.fomitepress.com/FOMITE/Our_Books.html

More Titles from Fomite...

Novels

Joshua Amses — *During This, Our Nadir*
Joshua Amses — *Ghatsr*
Joshua Amses — *Raven or Crow*
Joshua Amses — *The Moment Before an Injury*
Jaysinh Birjepatel — *Nothing Beside Remains*
Jaysinh Birjepatel — *The Good Muslim of Jackson Heights*
David Brizer — *Victor Rand*
Paula Closson Buck — *Summer on the Cold War Planet*
Dan Chodorkoff — *Loisaida*
David Adams Cleveland — *Time's Betrayal*
Jaimee Wriston Colbert — *Vanishing Acts*
Roger Coleman — *Skywreck Afternoons*
Marc Estrin — *Hyde*
Marc Estrin — *Kafka's Roach*
Marc Estrin — *Speckled Vanities*
Zdravka Evtimova — *In the Town of Joy and Peace*
Zdravka Evtimova — *Sinfonia Bulgarica*
Zdravka Evtimova — *You Can Smile on Wednesdays*
Peter Fortunato — *Carnevale*
Daniel Forbes — *Derail This Train Wreck*
Greg Guma — *Dons of Time*
Richard Hawley — *The Three Lives of Jonathan Force*
Lamar Herrin — *Father Figure*
Michael Horner — *Damage Control*
Ron Jacobs — *All the Sinners Saints*
Ron Jacobs — *Short Order Frame Up*
Ron Jacobs — *The Co-conspirator's Tale*
Scott Archer Jones — *And Throw Away the Skins*
Scott Archer Jones — *A Rising Tide of People Swept Away*
Julie Justicz — *Degrees of Difficulty*

Fomite

Maggie Kast — *A Free Unsullied Land*
Darrell Kastin — *Shadowboxing with Bukowski*
Coleen Kearon — *#triggerwarning*
Coleen Kearon — *Feminist on Fire*
Jan English Leary — *Thicker Than Blood*
Diane Lefer — *Confessions of a Carnivore*
Rob Lenihan — *Born Speaking Lies*
Douglas Milliken — *Our Shadow's Voice*
Colin Mitchell — *Roadman*
Ilan Mochari — *Zinsky the Obscure*
Peter Nash — *Parsimony*
Peter Nash — *The Perfection of Things*
George Ovitt — *Stillpoint*
George Ovitt — *Tribunal*
Gregory Papadoyiannis — *The Baby Jazz*
Pelham — *The Walking Poor*
Andy Potok — *My Father's Keeper*
Frederick Ramey — *Comes A Time*
Joseph Rathgeber — *Mixedbloods*
Kathryn Roberts — *Companion Plants*
Robert Rosenberg — *Isles of the Blind*
Fred Russell — *Rafi's World*
Ron Savage — *Voyeur in Tangier*
David Schein — *The Adoption*
Lynn Sloan — *Principles of Navigation*
L.E. Smith — *The Consequence of Gesture*
L.E. Smith — *Travers' Inferno*
L.E. Smith — *Untimely RIPped*
Bob Sommer — *A Great Fullness*
Tom Walker — *A Day in the Life*
Susan V. Weiss —*My God, What Have We Done?*
Peter M. Wheelwright — *As It Is On Earth*
Suzie Wizowaty — *The Return of Jason Green*

Poetry
Anna Blackmer — *Hexagrams*
Antonello Borra — *Alfabestiario*
Antonello Borra — *AlphaBetaBestiaro*
Antonello Borra — *Fabbrica delle idee/The Factory of Ideas*
L. Brown — *Loopholes*
Sue D. Burton — *Little Steel*
David Cavanagh— *Cycling in Plato's Cave*
James Connolly — *Picking Up the Bodies*
Greg Delanty — *Loosestrife*
Mason Drukman — *Drawing on Life*
J. C. Ellefson — *Foreign Tales of Exemplum and Woe*
Tina Escaja/Mark Eisner — *Caida Libre/Free Fall*
Anna Faktorovich — *Improvisational Arguments*
Barry Goldensohn — *Snake in the Spine, Wolf in the Heart*
Barry Goldensohn — *The Hundred Yard Dash Man*

Fomite

Barry Goldensohn — *The Listener Aspires to the Condition of Music*
R. L. Green — *When You Remember Deir Yassin*
Gail Holst-Warhaft — *Lucky Country*
Raymond Luczak — *A Babble of Objects*
Kate Magill — *Roadworthy Creature, Roadworthy Craft*
Tony Magistrale — *Entanglements*
Gary Mesick — *General Discharge*
Andreas Nolte — *Mascha: The Poems of Mascha Kaléko*
Sherry Olson — *Four-Way Stop*
Brett Ortler — *Lessons of the Dead*
Aristea Papalexandrou/Philip Ramp — Μας προσπερνά/*It's Overtaking Us*
Janice Miller Potter — *Meanwell*
Janice Miller Potter — *Thoreau's Umbrella*
Philip Ramp — *The Melancholy of a Life as the Joy of Living It Slowly Chills*
Joseph D. Reich — *A Case Study of Werewolves*
Joseph D. Reich — *Connecting the Dots to Shangrila*
Joseph D. Reich — *The Derivation of Cowboys and Indians*
Joseph D. Reich — *The Hole That Runs Through Utopia*
Joseph D. Reich — *The Housing Market*
Kenneth Rosen and Richard Wilson — *Gomorrah*
Fred Rosenblum — *Vietnumb*
Fred Rosenblum — *Playing Chicken with an Iron Horse*
David Schein — *My Murder and Other Local News*
Harold Schweizer — *Miriam's Book*
Scott T. Starbuck — *Carbonfish Blues*
Scott T. Starbuck — *Hawk on Wire*
Scott T. Starbuck — *Industrial Oz*
Seth Steinzor — *Among the Lost*
Seth Steinzor — *To Join the Lost*
Susan Thomas — *In the Sadness Museum*
Susan Thomas — *The Empty Notebook Interrogates Itself*
Paolo Valesio/Todd Portnowitz — *La Mezzanotte di Spoleto/Midnight in Spoleto*
Sharon Webster — *Everyone Lives Here*
Tony Whedon — *The Tres Riches Heures*
Tony Whedon — *The Falkland Quartet*
Claire Zoghb — *Dispatches from Everest*

Stories
MaryEllen Beveridge — *After the Hunger*
MaryEllen Beveridge — *Permeable Boundaries*
Jay Boyer — *Flight*
L. M Brown — *Treading the Uneven Road*
Michael Cocchiarale — *Here Is Ware*
Michael Cocchiarale — *Still Time*
Neil Connelly — *In the Wake of Our Vows*
Catherine Zobal Dent — *Unfinished Stories of Girls*
Zdravka Evtimova —*Carts and Other Stories*
John Michael Flynn — *Off to the Next Wherever*
Derek Furr — *Semitones*
Derek Furr — *Suite for Three Voices*

Fomite

Elizabeth Genovise — *Where There Are Two or More*
Andrei Guriuanu — *Body of Work*
Zeke Jarvis — *In A Family Way*
Arya Jenkins — *Blue Songs in an Open Key*
Jan English Leary — *Skating on the Vertical*
Marjorie Maddox — *What She Was Saying*
William Marquess — *Boom-shacka-lacka*
Gary Miller — *Museum of the Americas*
Jennifer Anne Moses — *Visiting Hours*
Martin Ott — *Interrogations*
Christopher Peterson — *Amoebic Simulacra*
Jack Pulaski — *Love's Labours*
Charles Rafferty — *Saturday Night at Magellan's*
Ron Savage — *What We Do For Love*
Fred Skolnik — *Americans and Other Stories*
Lynn Sloan — *This Far Is Not Far Enough*
L.E. Smith — *Views Cost Extra*
Caitlin Hamilton Summie — *To Lay To Rest Our Ghosts*
Susan Thomas — *Among Angelic Orders*
Tom Walker — *Signed Confessions*
Silas Dent Zobal — *The Inconvenience of the Wings*

Odd Birds
William Benton — *Eye Contact: Writing on Art*
Micheal Breiner — *the way none of this happened*
J. C. Ellefson — *Under the Influence: Shouting Out to Walt*
David Ross Gunn — *Cautionary Chronicles*
Andrei Guriuanu and Teknari — *The Darkest City*
Gail Holst-Warhaft — *The Fall of Athens*
Roger Lebovitz — *A Guide to the Western Slopes and the Outlying Area*
Roger Lebovitz — *Twenty-two Instructions for Near Survival*
dug Nap— *Artsy Fartsy*
Delia Bell Robinson — *A Shirtwaist Story*
Peter Schumann — *Belligerent & Not So Belligerent Slogans from the Possibilitarian Arsenal*
Peter Schumann — *Bread & Sentences*
Peter Schumann — *Children's Deprimer*
Peter Schumann — *Charlotte Salomon*
Peter Schumann — *Diagonal Man Theory + Praxis, Volumes One and Two*
Peter Schumann — *Faust 3*
Peter Schumann — *Planet Kasper, Volumes One and Two*
Peter Schumann — *We*

Plays
Stephen Goldberg — *Screwed and Other Plays*
Michele Markarian — *Unborn Children of America*

Essays
Robert Sommer — *Losing Francis: Essays on the Wars at Home*

When I read Birhan Keskin's poems I hear an oud playing a double makam: the one a fixed, the other a spontaneous/improvisatory mode. In filigree, the fixed is rooted in the poetic archetypes of Layla & Majnun, the Persian poem of love, loss and spiritual redemption,—except that here we no longer know who is majnun, i.e. crazy or possessed—while the spontaneous/improvisatory makes language boil over, literally makes it become concrete (as in "concrete poetry"). Or is it that the written is silently sounded & the sounded silently written? There is a quest going on here, a quest for a visionary but a-religious spirituality, encapsulated in the title itself, *Y'ol*, "the road to becoming." I cannot help but think of a lineage that reaches from Rabia of Basra, the first mystic Sufi woman poet to a contemporary such as Adonis. Only a poet-translator of Murat Nemet-Nejat's linguistic dexterity & depth of knowledge could have accomplished the tour-de-force of transposing this work into English.
PIERRE JORIS

"the other calls the one who isn't there / that's how magic becomes magic"—there's no getting around it. To live is to desire, thus, ultimately to anguish. In *Y'ol*, the world is unstable, even untrustworthy. But this only makes love more important: "the sky i return, return return / return to is you". Love—defined in these poems through an endless yearning—could have been denied but instead is upheld, even as these poems of fortitude must scorch their pages. The title "Y'ol" means "the road of/ towards becoming." This *Y'ol* presents the jagged music of metamorphosis and to read these poems is to discern songs made possible only with silence set on fire.
EILEEN TABIOS

Birhan Keskin's *Y'ol* is a singular accomplishment, a book about desire and loss and craziness on a grand scale, the Turkish equivalent, perhaps, of something like Nicole Brossard's *Mauve Desert*. Keskin's lovers break the bonds of sentence construction and even numerical order with the fury of the "retained and detained"—one long poem in numbered sections makes a muddle of the numbers themselves, as though the individual pieces had been scattered across the pages like dice from a dice cup. Its passion fairly takes away the breath of the reader, and Murat Nemet-Nejat's nimble translation captures nuance as well as it brings us the flesh and blood of two women playing for keeps across an erotic landscape unlike any other I've seen in contemporary poetry.
KEVIN KILLIAN

I'm a gone and committed fan of what's happening in Birhan Keskin's *Y'ol*. It shakes me up in my writing, heart and mind. It's in my day. Its flow is nakedly experiential, yet its unquestionably operating out of the profound blindness of poetry, language reaches for a place. These verses are dirty like the road of love. Immediately I read Y'ol with all of me, felt challenged and pulled like watching an amazing athlete or yoga practitioner going through their steps and yet it's the nature of this art form to move and tear and go forward into nothing. It's a virtuosic dance and a collapse, a reminder and a revelation. Every lover becomes her "us."
EILEEN MYLES